The RV Centennial Cookbook

ISBN 978-1-934302-88-0 (hardback)

TSTC Publishing
Texas State Technical College Waco
3801 Campus Drive
Waco, Texas 76705
http://publishing.tstc.edu/

Publisher: Mark Long
Project manager: Sheila Boggess
Art director: Stacie Buterbaugh
Sales manager: Wes Lowe
Indexing: Michelle Graye, indexing@yahoo.com
Editorial interns: Dannyele Wilson and Stori Long

Book design
Cecilia Sorochin ~ SoroDesign

This book was typeset in Berkeley Oldstyle Book
combined with the Din family.

Printed in China through Asia Pacific Offset
First edition, second printing

Publisher's Cataloging-in-Publication
(Provided by Quality Books, Inc.)

Cooper, Evada.
    The RV centennial cookbook : celebrating 100
    years of RVing / Evada Cooper.
    p. cm.
    Includes index.
    ISBN-13: 978-1-934302-88-0
    ISBN-10: 1-934302-88-0

    1. Cookbooks. 2. Recreational vehicle camping.
    I. Title.
    TX714.C66 2011   641.5
                    QBI10-600234

The RV Centennial Cookbook

CELEBRATING 100 YEARS OF RVING

Evada Cooper

TABLE OF

CONTENTS

DESSERTS · 104

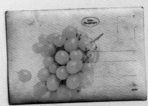

PREFACE

From the
RECREATION VEHICLE INDUSTRY ASSOCIATION

I'd like to invite you to celebrate 100 years of RVing with this cookbook by Evada Cooper, endorsed by the Recreation Vehicle Industry Association (RVIA) as the official cookbook of the RV Industry Centennial Celebration. *The RV Centennial Cookbook: Celebrating 100 Years of RVing* offers more than just easy-to-assemble recipes; it also has RV maintenance tips, a list of RV organizations, historical nuggets chronicling RV history, and instructions on playing family games of yesteryear.

RVIA has designated an industry-wide, year-long celebration to recognize the industry and the pioneering spirit that continues to drive the industry today. It is dedicated to those who are the heart and soul of our industry's success: the RV workers. These hard-working men and women provide the elbow grease and take special pride in their work. Many come from generations of families who work in this industry, all of them committed to building the best product they can.

The RV industry began in 1910 when the first mass-produced, manufactured auto campers and camping trailers—the forerunners of today's RVs—were built. Please visit GoRVing.com to see why these all-American products captured the heart of the nation and continue to do so.

Enjoy!

Richard Coon

RVIA President

INTRODUCTION

Think back to your first camping trip … the smell of food cooking over the campfire while adults visit, children playing Kick the Can nearby, and fireflies flickering in the night sky. The sounds of locusts, grasshoppers, crickets, and an occasional croaking frog dance together in harmony with nature, broken by the sounds of laughter everywhere.

The more technological advances have allowed people to get up and go, the more people have sought to return to the simple things in life. As the automobile created the need for unending ribbons of highways, the yearning to explore and return to nature helped to create the recreation vehicle industry more than a century ago.

This cookbook, *The RV Centennial Cookbook: Celebrating 100 Years of RVing*, commemorates the lifestyle and spirit of those who take to the road in a recreation vehicle. A dash of historical nuggets wrap around a vast array of recipes. Check out page 126 to find out what year the first RV made its debut. Of course, that was long after the first RVers carved trails to the west in their covered wagons. Cooking "on the road" was a necessity back then.

But back to those recipes. Evada Cooper has collected recipes far and wide from avid RVers. They are divided into the following categories: Appetizers, Entrees, Side Dishes, and Desserts.

"It's all about family, friends, and food," said Cooper. "My Favorite Taco Salad" (see page 49) made in a food-safe trash bag is only one of many easy-to-assemble recipes to share with RV neighbors for life on the road.

And when it comes to motorized coaches, life on the road sometimes includes breakdowns. Cooper's husband, Terry, known as the Texas RV Professor, shares an array of maintenance tips to keep your RV in tiptop shape. For example, do you know that regulators are not repairable? See page 54 to learn more about this.

We also sprinkled instructions on how to play favorite outdoor games throughout the book. Whether it's Kick the Can, Freeze Tag, or Marco Polo, adults will have as much fun teaching the games to youngsters as when they played the games years ago.

Whether it's eating, fishing, or visiting, RVers just enjoy spending time together. At the back of this book, you'll find a vast list of RV organizations. There also are national organizations such as the Recreation Vehicle Industry Association (RVIA) and ones that represent RVers in Canada.

So with all the information, tips, recipes, and games packed in this book, be sure to grab it as you board your RV. Happy travels to wherever your RV takes you!

Appetizers

$1,000 WINNER

Ingredients

apples
strawberries
banana
pineapple
1 jar of Smucker's caramel ice cream topping
1 package (8 oz.) cream cheese

Instructions

Use the microwave to soften the caramel ice cream topping and cream cheese, just enough to mix. Put in center of a multiple space serving dish. Surround with all the fruit. Use tooth picks in order to dip.

Theresa Faylene Wolcott, Harriman, Tenn.

We purchased our first RV in 1994. It was a 32-foot plain Jane. We kept it for one year and upgraded to a 37-foot J Pace Arrow, with all the trimmings. We belong to the Camping World RVers. We bought our RV because we have two daughters and six grandchildren, and we went on every vacation together for ten years. The guys sleep in tents. But during the time when we are all inside, we have to love each and every one really well. We all love it; our children are always making new friends, swimming, or whatever is available. We have no schedule due to the stress of timekeeping so when everyone is ready, we count off and leave. Oh, did I tell you we have 12 people in our rig? So if you walk by, and the RV is rocking, please knock on the door. You are more than welcome to say, "Hey, quiet please, you are disturbing the rest of us."

ARTICHOKES APPETIZER

Ingredients

2 cans artichoke hearts
2 T. mayonnaise
1 C. parmesan cheese
1 T. parmesan cheese
crackers

Instructions

Drain the cans of artichokes and place in bowl. Using a fork, smash the artichokes into smaller pieces. Next, mix in the mayonnaise; add in the cup of parmesan cheese. At the end, sprinkle the tablespoon of parmesan cheese on top. Bake in the oven or convection oven at 375 degrees for 45 minutes to 1 hour or until the cheese on top turns to a light brown. Serve with crackers. This is a crowd pleaser and will go quickly. For best results, serve hot.

Bev Overbey, Cincinnati, Ohio

We have been RVing and Workamping for five years in our 37-foot Georgetown Motor Home. We are members of Workamper News, KOA, Thousand Trails, and FMCA. We have seen a lot of the country, and because of this have collected pictures, stories, and other information. I started a website (www.Todaysrv.com) sharing my experiences and knowledge to help others.

BEANS WITH BACON DIP

Ingredients

1 large can Campbell's Beans with Bacon Soup
2 small cans Ro★Tel diced green chilies (you decide if you want the hot ones)
3 diced shallots
2 ½ C. shredded cheese
1 C. water
dash of salt, if desired
1 large bag tortilla chips

Instructions

Dump soup in 2 qt. sauce pan. Add water, chilies, shallots, and salt. Heat until warm and bubbly. Slowly add cheese till it is all melted in and creamy. Serve warm with chips.

Kandee Sebelius, Sparks, Nev.

I have been RVing more than 30 years. We started out with a 1976 Itasca and three kids, and upgraded to a 1995 Itasca. Now we own a 2008 Discovery and live full time in it. My husband and I have been full-timers for 3 years now and love it. We wanted to travel, but the economy hasn't let us get out there yet. We belong to Good Sam Club and KOA. We managed the park in which we are currently located for a few months, while the regular manager took some time off, and loved it. We would like to meet more people. We have nine grandkids, so we love children and would like to help families have a safe camping trip. We also have a Jack Russell terrier named Cody, who currently is the light of our home. I have almost completed the Lewis and Clark trail by RV (I love history stuff). I am a certified canoeist, master food preserver, school bus driver, creator of stained glass, and gardener. My hubby loves music, movies, gardening, and meeting new people.

What is an RV?

RV stands for recreation vehicle. In some states and other countries, it is called a caravan or a camper van. It is a vehicle fully equipped with a kitchen, bathroom, beds, dining area, and living area.

CAMPFIRE ONION

Ingredients

1 large onion
1 T. olive oil
1 T. Worchestershire sauce
Texas Pete hot sauce (to taste)
Season All or Old Bay crab seasoning

Instructions

Slice onion like cutting a pie almost to the bottom of the onion. Place on a sheet of aluminum foil that will cover the onion when folded up around it. Dribble olive oil and Worcestershire sauce on top of onion. Add several drops of Texas Pete hot sauce if desired. Sprinkle Season All seasoned salt or Old Bay crab seasoning to top of onion. Fold aluminum foil up and around the onion and twist excess to keep steam inside while onion is on grill. Onion is done when it can be mashed with bottom of fork or spoon. Be careful of hot steam when opening foil.

Huck Hutchens, Weslaco, Texas

My wife, Peggy, and I lived in our 1988 36-foot Overland or 1999 Holiday Rambler for 10 years, traveling around the U.S. and Canada, spending our winters in the Rio Grande Valley. In 2004, we bought a permanent mobile home in a retirement community in Weslaco, Texas. We kept our motor home, and now use it as a second home as Park Host at Estero Llano Grande SP/WBC in Weslaco. While full-time camping, we belonged to Escapees and have been members of Coast to Coast and Passport America since 1988. It is a great lifestyle and full of wonderful experiences.

HOT ARTICHOKE CRABMEAT DIP

Ingredients

1 package (8 oz.) cream cheese, softened
¼ C. mayonnaise
1 garlic clove, pressed
1 can (14 oz.) artichoke hearts in water, drained and chopped
1 package (8 oz.) imitation crabmeat, chopped (1 ½ C.)
¼ C. (3 oz.) grated fresh parmesan cheese
⅓ C. thinly sliced green onions with tops
zest of 1 lemon (1 t.)
⅓ t. ground black pepper
⅓ C. chopped red bell pepper

Instructions

Pre-heat oven to 350 degrees. Combine cream cheese and mayonnaise. Mix well. Press garlic into mixture. Drain artichokes; chop and mix with crabmeat. Combine parmesan cheese, green onions, and lemon zest. Mix all ingredients together and add to cream cheese mixture. Spoon mixture into a 1 ½ qt. baking dish. Bake 25 to 30 minutes or until golden brown around the edges. Sprinkle with red bell pepper and additional green onions.

Virginia Praesel, Rochdale, Texas

Our children loved camping when our family was young. I did lots of cooking for them during our summer outings. Now that they are all grown, they take their children RVing. In fact, most of my children now have RVs.

HOT PRETZEL STICKS

SWING THE STATUE

This game can be wildly funny, but supervision is needed to be sure the game doesn't get out of hand. Break players into teams of 2 players each. A player from each team takes his partner's hand and swings her round, then lets go of her hand. However she lands, she must freeze in that position. The player who loses balance, or moves and breaks the freeze, loses for the team. The team whose player remains motionless the longest as a statue wins the game for the team.

Ingredients

½ envelope ranch dressing mix
½ t. garlic powder
½ t. ground red pepper
½ C. oil
1 bag pretzel sticks

Instructions

Combine all ingredients except pretzels. Place the pretzels in a shallow pan. Pour the mixture over pretzels and mix until well coated. Bake in oven at 200 degrees for 1 hour.

Michelle, Tivoli, Texas

My husband and I have been RVing for many years. We lived full time in our motor home for a few years while my husband attended college. Now that he has finished and started his own business, we now live back in a brick and stick home; however, we will always love RVing and go every chance we get.

JALAPENO POPPER DIP

Ingredients

1 can (4 oz.) chopped jalapenos
1 can (4 oz.) chopped green chilies
1 tub (16 oz.) cream cheese
1 tub (16 oz.) grated parmesan cheese

Instructions

Dump it all together and mix it up. Heat it up until smooth and bubbly. This recipe can be baked if you have an oven available. Serve with tortilla chips or corn chips. This recipe really does taste like jalapeno poppers and is much easier to prepare and serve!

Janice Fischer, full-time RVer

My husband and I have been on the road for five years with no intention of giving it up. We drive and live in our 38-foot Newmar Mountain Aire which has all the conveniences of a house with a foundation. We belong to a variety of organizations catering to RVers including FMCA and Good Sam Club. Once a year we meet up with friends in Quartzsite, Arizona, to share food and frivolity for a week. Occasionally we join up with another couple for a month or two of travel. Life has been good for us along the side roads of America!

PERSONAL PARTY PIZZA

Ingredients

1 loaf pita bread or Earth Grain thin buns
1 ¼ C. chunky Ragu pasta sauce or brand of
  your choice
1 C. shredded mozzarella cheese
1 small onion, chopped fine
½ medium bell pepper, chopped fine
4 oz. ripe olives, chopped
4 oz. fresh mushrooms, chopped, or you may use
  canned mushrooms (not as good)
The following may be added to taste/preference:
  ¼ lb. to ½ lb. cooked hamburger, crumbled
  sliced pepperoni and/or
  cooked and crumbled sausage

Instructions

Split pita bread or thin buns in half, place crust side down on a large cookie sheet. Spread 1 T. pasta sauce on each half. Sprinkle on cheese. Add any other topping you may prefer. Place in 400 degree oven for 8 to 10 minutes or until cheese is melted and edge of crust is crisp. This is best served hot. One package of pita bread or Earth Grain thin buns makes 16 pizzas.

Barbara Spriggs, Somerville, Texas

My son is the Texas RV Professor, Terry Cooper. My RVing history is proudly watching him excel in his profession.

PICO DE GALLO

Ingredients

1 small can black olives, drained
4 Roma tomatoes
4 green onions with tops
2 jalapeno peppers, seeded
1 ½ T. olive oil
1 t. vinegar
1 t. garlic salt

Instructions

Chop into small pieces the first four ingredients. Mix oil, vinegar, and garlic salt and pour over chopped ingredients. Mix well and serve. This recipe will last in the refrigerator up to a week.

tech tip

Batteries are like piggy banks. We have to put something in them in order to get something out. Have you charged your batteries lately?

Becky, Milano, Texas

I have been an avid RVer since I was a little girl. I loved going on trips with my dad and older sister. I have great family memories of that special time in my life.

TACO DIP

Ingredients

8 oz. cream cheese
1 package dry taco seasoning mix (such as McCormick's)
½ C. sour cream
salsa sauce
shredded lettuce
sliced black olives
shredded Monterey jack or cheddar cheese
sour cream
guacamole

Instructions

Beat together cream cheese, sour cream, and taco seasoning until completely blended. Spread on flat dish and top with remaining ingredients, as much or little as you like. Serve with tortilla chips.

Carolyn Barfield, Pacific, Mo.

My husband and I have been RVing since 1990, when we started with a really small used travel trailer. We loved that old trailer, but stepped up in a few years to a 5th wheel and a small Class B camper. We also acquired two small dogs who love to travel. They begin getting excited when they see us loading up the camper. We are in our twelfth year of volunteer hosting in Missouri State Parks. We have also volunteered at parks in Maryland and Virginia, which we found out about through Workamper News. As we host in the parks, it gives us the opportunity to meet a variety of people from all over the U.S. and Canada. We have met some great friends hosting and traveling, and still try to see them at least once a year if not more often. We have five children, seven grandchildren and four great-grandchildren, and will try to keep camping as long as our health holds out. We recommend RVing to anyone and everyone.

Side Dishes

APPLE CORNBREAD

Ingredients

1 C. cornmeal
1 C. flour
⅓ C. brown sugar
3 t. baking powder
1 t. salt
1 C. milk
1 egg, beaten
¼ C. shortening, melted
1 apple, finely diced (I peel ours, but you can leave it unpeeled if you have organic apples)

Instructions

Mix dry ingredients; set aside. In another bowl, combine milk, egg, and shortening. (You may want to warm the milk slightly to keep the shortening from clumping back up, but not too much or you'll cook the egg.) Add cornmeal mixture to wet ingredients. Add apple and stir gently; batter will be very thick. Pour into greased 9x9 pan and bake in the oven at 425 degrees for 20-25 minutes. To make sure it cooks through in the middle, since it is a heavier-than-usual cornbread batter, you may want to check about 20 minutes–if the center still seems uncooked, cover with foil to prevent overbrowning and increase cook time as needed.

Marlene Wenger, Grafton, W. Va.

We belong to Cedar Creek RV Club. We have been RVers since 1997. Our first unit was a small Class C Coachman, and then we had a Class C Fourwinds from 2000 to 2009. We love our new unit, a 2008 37CKQS Cedar Creek Custom, pulled by 2007 Chevy Silverado 3500. We plan on enjoying our retirement on the road and expanding our camping family. God bless and safe travels!

BACON RANCH POTATOES

Ingredients

2 large baking potatoes
½ C. bacon bits
1 bottle (12 oz.) ranch dressing
1 C. shredded cheese of your choice
(you can add more if desired)

Instructions

Peel potatoes and cut into chunks. Bring them to a boil on stove top and boil just long enough to be fork tender, not mushy. Drain and place in 8x8 baking pan. Sprinkle the bacon bits, pour the ranch dressing over top, and cover with shredded cheese. Bake in oven at 350 degrees just until the cheese is melted. Serve and enjoy! You can use fresh cooked bacon crumbled. Shredded fiesta cheese works well with this also.

Lill, Paragould, Ark.

We started work camping in 1973. We didn't know there was anything called work camping at that time, but have done it ever since. Our first RV was a tent, which we set up in the dark of night with no flashlight. Our night was not that restful. We woke up the next morning to find we had been sleeping in sleeping bags on a bed of walnuts. We laughed the next morning about how anyone could be that dumb. Needless to say, we immediately bought a flashlight and have never forgotten one since. We now own a Class A motor home camper. We belong to Camp Club USA and Passport America, and we are lifetime members of Good Sam Club.

Lianne Vipond, Sault Ste. Marie, Ontario, Canada

This recipe was given to me by Priscilla Ninedorf. She and her husband, Fritz, were full-timers for the past 20 years and were members of Escapees. I met Priscilla when we work camped together in Texas. In 2009, when she was 71 years old and after a year of mourning Fritz's death, she decided to get back out on the road by herself in a 36-foot Allegro Bay towing a Saturn station wagon. Priscilla was sweet, funny, and tough! She broke her arm and shoulder when mopping the floor one day and instead of complaining, she put the phone on speaker and continued to take reservations! She loved to golf and was able to get back into the game after her arm healed. Priscilla and Fritz had traveled all over the United States and she kept us laughing with stories of their travels. She shared her knowledge about where to go, what to see, etc. and our travels have been greatly enhanced because of her advice. Priscilla passed away in January 2010, and will be greatly missed by all her friends.

BEER BREAD

Ingredients

5-5 ½ C. flour
2 packages yeast
¼ C. sugar
1 ½ t. salt
½ C. water
1 ½ C. (12 oz.) beer
3 T. cooking oil
cornmeal

Instructions

Combine 2 C. flour, yeast, sugar, and salt. Mix well. Heat water, beer, and oil until warm (120-130 degrees). Add to flour mixture. Blend at low mixer speed until moist. Beat 3 minutes at medium speed. By hand, gradually stir in remaining flour to make a soft dough. Knead until smooth and elastic (about 5 minutes). Place in a greased bowl, turning to grease top also. Cover, let rise until light and double in bulk (about 1 hour). Punch down dough. Divide into 2 parts. On lightly floured surface, roll or pat to a 7x11 inch rectangle. Start with the longer side and roll up tightly. Place seam-side down on a greased cookie sheet sprinkled with cornmeal. With a sharp knife, make 3 or 4 diagonal slashes across the top. Cover and let rise until double (½-¾ hour). Bake in oven at 375 degrees for 30-35 minutes.

BEER BREAD

Ingredients

2 C. self-rising flour
12 oz. beer (room temperature)
3 T. sugar
Variations:
　1 C. shredded cheese
　½ C. grated onion

Instructions

Set oven on 375 degrees; mix flour and sugar in mixing bowl. Add beer; stir with spatula till flour is moistened completely. If desired, add cheese and/or onion at this point. Pour into greased bread pan. Bake 40-45 minutes until top is lightly brown and pulls away from sides and toothpick inserted in center comes out clean. Cool in pan on wire rack for 5 minutes, then invert on rack to cool. Butter top, bottom, sides, and ends while cooling; this will keep the crust soft.

Ann Griffey, Shelbyville, Ind.

I have belonged to RVing Women Ohio River Valley Chapter for 4 years.

BLACK & WHITE BEAN SALAD

Ingredients

1 can black beans
1 can white beans
½ red onion
parsley
¼ C. olive oil
2 T. balsamic vinegar
salt and pepper to taste

Teardrop RV?

Teardrops are among the earliest RV designs, and are considered vintage no matter the number of years.

Instructions

Drain and rinse the beans. Chop red onion and parsley. Mix all ingredients together. Can be served cold or at room temperature. Best if made several hours or 1 day in advance.

Johanna Kashi, Petersburg, Va.

We became full-time RVers 3 years ago. We travel in a 33-foot Class A along with our chocolate lab mix, Mocha. So far we have work camped in Louisiana, Florida, Virginia, and Maine. We have both volunteered and worked for pay.

BUTTERMILK SALAD

tech tip

We purchase propane as a liquid and consume it as a gas. Propane expands 270 times when it boils and goes from a liquid to a gas.

Ingredients

1 C. buttermilk
1 tub (8 oz.) Cool Whip
1 small box instant vanilla pudding
1 can (20 oz.) crushed pineapple, drained
1 big can mandarin oranges, drained
½ package Keebler Fudge Deluxe Graham
   Cookies, crumbled

Instructions

Mix together buttermilk, Cool Whip, and vanilla pudding. Add the pineapple and oranges. Mix well. Chill until ready to serve. Add cookies just before serving.

Yvonne Baker, College Station, Texas

When I was a child, my siblings and I would go RVing with my grandparents. We loved it. Later, after growing up, my sister and I would take our families together on RVing trips while our children were young. That was many years ago. Now our children are doing the same thing with their children. Our family has had a wonderful history with RVing. I'm sure it will continue all because of the love of RVing our grandparents had all those years ago.

CABBAGE & BACON SKILLET

Ingredients

1 lb. bacon
1 head of cabbage
1 small onion
salt and pepper
water

Instructions

On stove top or over campfire in a heavy skillet, fry the bacon to almost crisp; take bacon out of skillet. Set aside. Drain some of grease out of pan, but not all. Cut up cabbage and put in skillet; add onion, about 1 C. of water, and salt and pepper to taste. Put heavy lid on skillet and simmer on medium heat until cabbage is soft. Check at times; stir and add more water as needed, or add some of the bacon grease if needed. Break up the bacon and put back into skillet with cabbage. Simmer about 10 minutes with lid on, and it's ready to serve.

Paul Meicher, Sioux Falls, S.D.

We have been RVing for 8 years and have a Class A motor home. We have belonged to FMCA for 3 years, Good Sam Club for 6 years, Escapees for 8 years, Passport America for 3 years, and Camping World for 8 years.

CAMPFIRE DUMP BEANS

Ingredients

1 can black beans, drained
1 can pinto beans, drained
1 can pork and beans, drained
1 can ranch style beans, drained
3 T. chopped bell pepper
3 T. chopped onions
1 T. mustard
1 T. ketchup
1 t. Worcestershire sauce
3 T. brown sugar
1 T. butter
1 t. Tony's seasoning (if you like the spice)

Instructions

Stir together butter and last 7 or 8 ingredients in microwave safe baking dish. Cover and microwave on high for 2 minutes (onions should be translucent). Uncover and add drained beans. Cover with a paper towel and microwave on high for an additional 5 minutes. These are great for a group. Just add additional cans to expand this when unexpected guests arrive. Great with barbecue, steaks, and chicken, and leftovers can be a complete meal if you simply add a little sausage or seasoned ground meat and serve with cornbread.

Diana LeBlanc, Houston, Texas

I have been with PPL Motor Homes in Houston since 1980, and have recently gotten more involved than ever with RVing. Grandkids do make a difference. We love outdoor grilling and cast iron pot cooking when we're on the road; it becomes a family affair. From the main course to the s'mores, we enjoy the outdoor RV lifestyle.

CAMPFIRE POTATOES

Ingredients

6 medium potatoes
1 red bell pepper
1 green bell pepper
2 onions
salt and pepper
½ stick butter

Instructions

Slice potatoes in ¼-inch horizontal slices. Slice the peppers and onion lengthwise in thin strips. Melt butter and mix all ingredients in a bowl. Season with salt and pepper to taste, wrap in double foil, and grill on campfire or gas grill until brown.

Sara Baker, College Station, Texas

 I am an RVer but just 17 years old. I like helping my mom when we cook this recipe on the campfire. I remember us going with my aunt and cousins where we would RV in their pop-up trailer. We would stay at the Texas State Parks. What great fun we had!

HOW TO PLAY KICK THE CAN

This ageless outdoor game apparently has had a comeback in recent years, and a ball of some type may replace the traditional can. For nostalgia's sake, though, let's stick with the can. (Besides, kicking a ball that travels much farther than a can could prolong the game well past bedtime.)

Needed to play: A large can, and as many players as you can find—the more, the better. Remember, though, you have to have at least three.

Select someone to be "it," who then stands by the can that is placed in an open area. "It" counts to a predetermined number as players run and hide. Then the person who is "it" tries to find the other players. When he finds one, the race is on back to the can where he must jump over the can while yelling, "1-2-3 on John (name the player)." Then John must stay in a designated area for "caught" players. If John beats "it" back and kicks the can, then the game starts again with any caught players hiding once again. Other players also can sneak in and "kick the can," releasing all of the caught players. Once all the players are caught, the first person caught becomes "it," and another round begins.

CHAROOMS

Ingredients

1 bunch Swiss chard, chard, or rainbow chard
½ lb. sliced mushrooms
2 T. extra virgin olive oil
1 small onion, diced
1 T. diced garlic
salt and pepper
1 T. balsamic vinegar (optional)

Instructions

Rinse chard in water, cut out center stems, and tear into bite-size pieces. In a sauté pan on stove top, add oil, garlic, and onions; sauté slowly to avoid burning garlic. Add in mushrooms and sauté until brown and liquid is absorbed. Add salt and pepper. Add in torn chard; cover and cook until wilted. Taste for spices. Sprinkle with balsamic vinegar if desired. Serve.

Iris, Cedar Glen, Calif.

We have been camping for years and RVing for 6 years. We own a 32–foot Tioga named Effie! We belong to Thousand Trails, Good Sam Club, ROD, and KOA. We eat well when we travel and try to take advantage of the seasonal and local foods.

CREAM OF ASPARAGUS SOUP

Ingredients

1 bunch asparagus
a few slices onion
a few stalks celery
1 sweet potato
2 C. organic chicken broth
1 whole chicken
(cooked and de-boned)

Instructions

One hour before chicken is done in crock pot, add asparagus, onion, celery, and sweet potato on top. When cooked, puree the vegetables in a blender. Season as needed.

Linda Olson, Washougal, Wash.

Larry and I have traveled in our RV for more than 17 years. We began our journey in Portland, Oregon. We are retired electricians that used our RV as our home to travel where the work was in our field. We have spent winters in Oregon, Washington, Nevada, and California (San Jose). We now spend winters in Apache Junction, Arizona. It became a way of life. We have tried condo living in Florida, but did not care for the humidity. We love the West. I have been experimenting with recipes recently because of health issues. What I like about the asparagus soup is that you do not have to add milk or white potatoes. It's so simple with even leftovers.

GRANDMA'S HOT BACON DRESSING SALAD

Ingredients

1 large bag salad mix
1 package (12 oz.) bacon
¼ C. water
¼ C. apple cider vinegar
¾ C. sugar
1 egg
4 heaping T. Miracle Whip

Instructions

Make up your salad how you like it with tomatoes, onions, cucumbers, etc. (Although, it is good with just a bag of regular salad mix and nothing else.) Cut the bacon into inch-long pieces. Fry the bacon on the stove top or in a skillet over a campfire until just crispy. Drain off most of the grease and leave in the pan. In a small pot mix the rest of the ingredients and cook over medium-high heat till the mixture comes together and thickens. Get bacon back to hot and add mixture to it. Stir and bring to a boil, scraping the bottom of the pan to get all the goodies mixed together. Remove from stove and pour over salad. It won't look like much, but keep tossing the salad and it will coat the lettuce. Enjoy!

David Baney, Copperas Cove, Texas

I started camping 40 years ago with the U.S. Army, sleeping in the snow. Over the years, I have had most every style of RV there is, from a tent to a motor home. My wife, Jeannie, and I currently have a 2003 Alpenlite 5th wheel towed with a Dodge Ram 2500. We belong to the Texas Boomers, which we joined about a year ago. This is my kind of group: one that loves to eat.

GREEN CHILI CHEESY RICE

Ingredients

3 C. cooked white rice
8 oz. sour cream
2 cans (4 oz.) diced green chilies
1 C. grated cheddar/mozzarella cheese
1 C. pepper jack cheese

Instructions

Mix all ingredients together, place in a greased casserole dish, and bake in oven for 40 minutes at 375 degrees.

Beth Wannberg, Nampa, Idaho

We have been RVing for most of our lives. I started with my parents, and then my husband picked it up when we got married. We have a 5th wheel that is usually parked in Cascade, Idaho, all summer. Both of us have retired, and we plan on making many memories by becoming work campers.

GRILLED CABBAGE

Ingredients

1 large head of cabbage
heavy duty aluminum foil
spices
1 stick of margarine

Instructions

You will need large heavy duty aluminum foil. Tear off a large enough piece to cover the cabbage very well. Take your cabbage and core out the heart, being careful not to lose any fingers in the process. Once cored, add lots of spices to the cabbage. I prefer Cajun spices because they have a little heat. If you like it really spicy, add some more cayenne pepper. It just depends on what flavors you like and how much flavor you want. Take the stick of margarine and put in the hole where the core came out. Using the paper from it, squash it into the core hole. Wrap the cabbage tightly with the foil and bake in oven at 400 degrees or on grill or smoker for about an hour or until it is soft. Some cabbages take a little longer than others. I usually place it on a cookie sheet in case the margarine leaks out so I don't have a 3-alarm fire on my grill or a mess in my oven. Remove and put in a bowl and cut it up to serve. Enjoy.

David Baney, Copperas Cove, Texas

INCREDIBLY FATTENING MACARONI CASSEROLE

Ingredients

1 large package large elbow macaroni
1 large box Velveeta cheese (do not use the off brand)
1 package (16 oz.) bacon
1 large onion, chopped
3 stalks celery, chopped fine
2 cans Ro★Tel tomatoes (you can use plain diced tomatoes instead if you don't want the heat)

Instructions

Cook macaroni and drain. Fry bacon and save drippings. Sauté celery and onions in some of the saved bacon drippings. In the pot you cooked the macaroni in, stir in the macaroni, tomatoes, celery, onion, and crumpled fried bacon as well as the remaining saved drippings. Put all mixture in 9x13 Pyrex dish. Slice cheese in chunks to cover. Bake in oven at 325 degrees until melted, about 30 to 40 minutes. Do not let burn.

Carol Klug, McAllen, Texas

MARCO POLO

This water game is simple, though its history is less clear. Players get in the water and designate a player to be Marco. Marco closes his/her eyes and calls out "Marco." Players respond by saying "Polo." Marco follows the direction of the voices and tries tagging players, all the while calling out "Marco" and listening to "Polo" responses. Players must respond by saying "Polo" but then try to get out of Marco's way to avoid being tagged. When a person is tagged, that person becomes Marco and the game begins again.

MARINATED PEA SALAD

Ingredients

2 cans (17 oz.) early peas, drained
1 can (16 oz.) bean sprouts, drained
1 jar (4-6 oz.) pimentos, drained, chopped
4 stalks celery, chopped
1 medium onion, chopped
¾ C. vegetable oil
¾ C. vinegar
¾ C. sugar
1 t. dried basil
1 t. garlic powder
1 t. salt

Instructions

In large bowl, combine first 5 ingredients, toss lightly. In a covered container (jar, Pyrex, etc.) combine oil, vinegar, sugar, and seasonings. Cover and shake vigorously. Pour dressing over vegetables and toss lightly. Cover and chill 8-10 hours, or overnight. Serve in a lettuce-lined bowl, if desired. Serves 8.

Mary T. Sandstrom, San Francisco, Calif.

We have been RVing for 3 years. We travel in a Class C Itasca Cambria with a Smart4Two tow vehicle. We are members of Camp Club USA, Camping World, Coast-to-Coast, Escapees, FMCA, Flying J, Good Sam, KOA, Passport America, WIT, and Woodall's. We recently completed a 9-month trek from California to New York and back. Utilizing most of our memberships during our trip was most enjoyable.

MEXICAN HAYSTACK SALAD

Ingredients

This recipe is calculated for 30 people.
It can be adjusted for smaller or larger groups.

15-17 C. cooked rice (not Minute Rice)
3 large bags Fritos or corn chips
2 one-gallon cans Wolf Brand Chili
2 lbs. shredded lettuce
15-18 tomatoes, diced
2 ½ lbs. onions, diced
4 lbs. shredded cheese
2 large cans black or green olives
1 lb. pecans, chopped
2 large bags shredded coconut
1 gallon salsa

Instructions

Cook rice by stovetop method on package. Heat chili on stove or electric roaster. Assemble all ingredients into individual containers and line in the order to the right on a serving table. Everyone in the group may go down the serving line and layer their salad with the ingredients of their choice. Don't leave out the pecans and coconut—they add a fresh blend to a traditional taste!

Sandy Creekmore, Cypress, Texas

My husband and I have camped all of our married life, beginning with tent camping, moving up to traveling with a pop-up camper, and starting RVing with our first 5th wheel in 1995. I began to organize the Texas Boomers RV Club in October 2000 with four charter members. The group is affiliated with an RV website called www.iRV2.com, where we are moderators on that forum. The Texas Boomers have grown in membership to more than 135 from across the state and celebrated their 10th anniversary in 2010. The Texas Boomers host 9–12 rallies a year with an average attendance of 40–45 rigs each. I also have coordinated two National Rallies for www.irv2.com in Texas where members of the organization came from all across the nation for a week of fun activities.

MY FAVORITE TACO SALAD

Ingredients

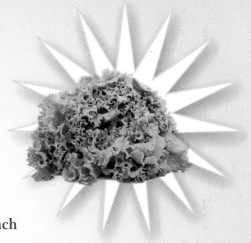

1 lb. hamburger
1 can kidney beans, drained
1 can garbanzo beans, drained
1 head lettuce, sliced thin and chopped
1 onion, chopped
1 lb. cheese, grated
1-2 tomatoes, chopped
1 package Doritos chips
1 bottle Kraft Creamy French Dressing (if
    you cannot find Kraft, find a creamy French
    dressing that tastes like it—this is the
    secret ingredient)

Instructions

Brown hamburger on stove top and drain thoroughly. Take a tall kitchen trash bag (food-safe, and not scented) and put all the ingredients in it, except the chips, tossing after you add each ingredient. The bag works great for tossing, and then you can put it in the fridge. It's great for transporting, and when you go to a party, you can curl back the edges and serve from the bag or transfer to a bowl. Just before you serve, dump the Doritos chips in. This salad is even better the next day. I even like to warm it a little to make it taste like a taco.

Linda Dean, New River, Ariz.

We have been in an RV off and on since 1982, living in a 32-foot Traveleze trailer for 9 years. We broke down and bought a house, but still had a cabover camper. Now we are back in the groove with a 31-foot Alpenlite that has been gently used.

RV Hall of Fame

The RV Hall of Fame is in Elkhart, Ind., and shares a library and museum with the Manufactured Housing (MH) Hall of Fame.

ONION CASSEROLE

Ingredients

4 C. sliced onions
1 can cream of mushroom soup
1 ¼ C. stuffing mix
1 stick oleo
½ C. sour cream

Instructions

Sauté onions in oleo until limp and clear. Combine all ingredients in casserole dish and bake in oven at 300 degrees for 30 minutes or until light brown.

Delilah Caven, Somerville, Texas

 I have always enjoyed RVing. Restoring the older units is where my love is.

POTATO SOUP

Ingredients

4 medium potatoes
½ medium white onion
1 t. salt
water
3 eggs
flour

Instructions

Peel, slice, and cube the potatoes and onion, and place in a medium pot. Add water, filling to 2 inches from top. Cook on medium-high heat until potatoes are soft. Increase heat until mixture is at a low boil. In a separate bowl, put 3 uncooked eggs. Combine flour with eggs until the mixture is a loose paste consistency. Add egg and flour mixture to soup by dropping it a little at a time from a fork. This mixture makes what my Grandmother called cone fleas, which is a type of dumpling. Continue cooking soup at a low boil until the cone fleas are cooked and not gummy. Soup should be served hot. Add a pat of butter and milk if desired. Crackers are a nice addition also.

Jim Gratz, Sebastopol, Texas

We have been RVing for more than 20 years, starting with a pop-up camper, and have spent the last 8 years in a 5th wheel. We are not full-timers, but any-timers, as we go when we want for as long as we want but still own a stick and brick home. We are members of Escapees, Thousand Trails, Western Horizons, Heartland Owners Club, Good Sam Club, Camp Club USA, Freedom Resorts, and Passport America. We love to attend RV rallies and have attended a number of them.

QUICK FRUIT SALAD

tech tip

Regulators are NOT repairable. They are inexpensive, so just replace them.

Ingredients

1 can pineapple chunks
1 can pears
1 jar (8 oz.) maraschino cherries
1 small package vanilla instant pudding mix
1 can peaches
3 large bananas
1 C. chopped pecans

Instructions

Drain all fruit, saving juices in one container. Cut up peaches and pears into size of pineapple chunks. Slice bananas, dice cherries, and combine all fruit. Add pecans. Sprinkle dry pudding mix over fruit and add 1 C. of mixed fruit juices. Stir well and refrigerate before serving.

Stephanie, Mesquite, Texas

My husband and I have a pop-up trailer and we enjoy weekend RVing with our two girls, 6 and 1 years old. I grew up going RVing with my parents, and I want to continue that tradition with my children. We are not in any RV clubs at this time, but will be in the future.

SHEILA'S CHEESY POTATO SOUP

Ingredients

6-7 medium potatoes, peeled and cubed
water to cover potatoes while cooking
1 pint sour cream (note: using fat-free sour cream does not make the soup as
    smooth, but it tastes the same and is healthier)
1 lb. Mexican Velveeta, cubed; regular Velveeta can be used, if preferred
real bacon bits (or crumble several slices of cooked bacon)
green onions, sliced

Instructions

Cover peeled, cubed potatoes with water in a large pot or Dutch oven. (Use more water for thinner soup.) When potatoes are tender, add sour cream and cubes of Velveeta. Heat over low heat, stirring. When cheese is melted, soup is ready. Add green onions and bacon bits just before serving.

Sheila Boggess, Prairie Hill, Texas

 Camping with neighbors in their pop-up RV is still one of my favorite memories.

SHOE PEG CORN SALAD

Ingredients

¼ C. white vinegar
1 can shoe peg corn, drained
1 can small peas, drained
1 jar (2 oz.) pimentos
8 green onions, chopped
1 bell pepper, chopped
1 can French cut green beans, drained
1 T. water
½ C. oil
1 C. sugar
1 t. salt
1 t. pepper
1 C. celery, chopped

Instructions

Bring vinegar, water, oil, and sugar to a boil. Cool. Mix vegetables. Pour liquid over vegetables. Place in tightly covered container and refrigerate 24 hours. Keeps very well.

Yvonne Baker, College Station, Texas

SLAW WITH CARAWAY & RAISINS

Ingredients

¾ C. sour cream
2 T. red wine vinegar
1 t. caraway seeds
½ t. salt
¼ t. pepper
4 C. thinly sliced green cabbage
3 large carrots, grated
1 ¼ C. golden raisins

Instructions

In a large bowl, whisk together the sour cream, vinegar, caraway seeds, salt, and pepper. Add cabbage, carrots, and raisins. Toss well and serve. Keeps well (covered) in the refrigerator for serving later. A great potluck dish!

Rachel Brett Harley, Ypsilanti, Mich.

For years, I was a backpacker and tent camper until 2001, when my back decided it was time to stop sleeping on the ground. So I bought my first 22-foot Trail-Lite B+ by R-Vision. I now own a 2009 28-foot Trail-Lite B named Vanna VanGo. I spend winters in my condo in Michigan and spend April through October on the road escaping summer's heat. I've driven to Alaska once and to Newfoundland three times. I credit four sessions of Life On Wheels with giving me the skills and information to be a savvy, safe RVer. I still keep in touch with a number of friends I've met in campgrounds all over the U.S. and Canada. Who says being a solo RVer is an experience of isolation? I've been a member of RVing Women (Great Lakers Chapter and Solos Chapter) since 2002. I also belong to Escapees and Good Sam Club. In July 2010, I hosted my first Great Lakers Chapter rally in Ishpeming, Michigan (in the UP). It's a themed rally: *Anatomy of a Murder*–51 Years Later.

SPUD SOUP

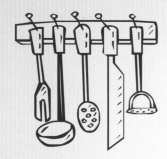

Ingredients

1 bag frozen hash browns, thawed
overnight in fridge
1 pint half & half
2 cans (10.5 oz.) cream of chicken soup
2 large cans Milnot (evaporated milk)
2 C. shredded mild cheddar cheese
1 stick butter
1 medium onion, chopped
salt and pepper to taste

Instructions

Melt the stick of butter in a sauce pan and sauté the onions until transparent. Mix all ingredients together and pour into crock pot. Cook on low for 6-8 hours or high for 3-4 hours.

Debbie Gleaves, Lawton, Okla.

Lee, my husband of 39 years, and I have owned different types of campers almost all of our married lives. Our current 36-foot Carriage is always ready to travel, but since we are not retired yet, it doesn't get out as often as it likes. I dream a lot as I read over the Workamper News opportunities, where I am a member, and read through the forums. Many hours are also spent keeping up with the Escapee news. Within Escapees, we are members of the BOF Christian Fellowship Group. We haven't made any of their meetings, but hope to soon.

SQUASH & APPLE BAKE

Ingredients

1 large butternut squash
3 large baking apples
1 stick butter
½ C. brown sugar
salt and pepper to taste

Instructions

Slice squash and apples into ½-inch slices. In baking dish, alternate layers of squash and apples, dotting each layer with butter and sprinkling with brown sugar, using salt and pepper to taste. Bake in oven at 350 degrees for 45-50 minutes.

tech tip

Ever have cold or warm water coming out of the hot side of your faucets? Check to see if someone has bumped the bypass valves on the back of your water heater.

Pat Jett

We have been full-timing for 7 years now in our 2003 Fleetwood Flair motor home. Using Workamper News, we have been lucky to find work in various parts of the United States and it has allowed us to live our dream. We also enjoy playing and singing country music for fellow RVers. Singing helped me get through the chemo treatments I needed in 2007. This recipe is great for potlucks, and by using a toss-away pan, I don't have to worry about getting my dish back.

STUFFED ONIONS

Ingredients

6 large onions of any type
2 C. cooked rice
¼ lb. ground beef or ground Italian sausage
seasonings

Instructions

Leaving the skins on the onions, cut off the root end, making a flat bottom. Cut off top of the onion and save it. Hollow out the onion, leaving about 3 layers on the outside. Combine rice with meat and seasonings and stuff into onions. Place tops back on onions and wrap in aluminum foil. Leave an opening at top for steam to come out. Place onions on grill and cook for about two hours or until very tender or cook over a campfire until done.

Pamela A. Praesel, Bryan, Texas

RV Games

HIDE-AND-SEEK

Many variations of this game exist. Choose someone to be "it," and that person counts to 100 or a predetermined number while all of the other players hide. (It's a good idea to go over rules before the game starts to indicate boundaries or if some places to hide are off-limits.) Once the person who is "it" finds someone, he calls out "1-2-3, I see John hiding behind the tree." John then must come to home base and wait for others to be found. One variation is when John is found, he and the person who is "it" race to home base. If John gets there first, he is safe. If he's tagged, he will be "it" for the next game if he's the first player caught. When "it" has found as many players as he can, he can call out, "Ally, ally, all come in free." Those still hiding then reveal themselves for a safe return home.

TORTILLA OR AZTEC SOUP

Ingredients

2 cans (13.5 oz.) chicken broth
1 can (15 oz.) black beans, drained and rinsed
1 can (11 oz.) Mexicali corn, drained
1 jar (11.5 oz.) of medium thick and chunky salsa
8 oz. cheddar cheese, grated
tortilla chips

Airstream Origins

Wally Byam is credited with using aluminum in trailer frames and skins like aircraft-type riveted bodies that became Airstream trailers. Byam, a lifetime RV lifestyle promoter, was inducted into the RV Hall of Fame in 1972 for his work as a pioneer trailer manufacturer and engineer.

Instructions

Put all ingredients except cheese and chips in pan on stove top. Bring to boil, and then simmer for 5 minutes. Put chips in bowl. Top with grated cheese. Spoon in soup.

Geraldine Johnson, Donna, Texas

We have RVed for many years, full time from 1989 through 1995.

YUMMY POTATO PACKETS

Ingredients

4 C. potatoes, thinly sliced, skins on
1 large onion, thinly sliced
2 cloves garlic, chopped fine (or garlic powder may be used)
4 pats butter or margarine
salt and pepper to taste
1 C. shredded cheddar cheese
red, yellow, and/or green peppers, sliced (optional)

Instructions

Divide and place potatoes, onions, and minced garlic evenly on 4 sheets of heavy duty aluminum foil. Place one butter pat on top of each. If not using minced garlic, sprinkle garlic powder and salt and pepper to taste. If desired, add optional red, yellow, and/or green peppers. These add flavor and color. Seal packets and place on hot grill for approximately 20-30 minutes, turning frequently to cook evenly. When done, open packets and sprinkle grated cheddar cheese on top. Serve and enjoy. Serves 4, but this recipe is easy to increase for a crowd. Note: After 15 minutes cooking time, packets can be placed on warming rack of grill to finish cooking while meat is cooking.

Normie, Arizona

We have lived full time in our 5th wheel for a little over 5 years. When I retired 2 years ago, we began traveling and work camping across the West and Southwest. We have worked in Texas, California, and Arizona, so far. We are originally from the Midwest and are enjoying the scenery and the sites, but most of all the lack of snow here in the West! We have a 34-foot 5th wheel with 3 slides and a one-ton dually tow vehicle, and travel with our 2 pups. We have been Escapees and Good Sam Club members for 5 years.

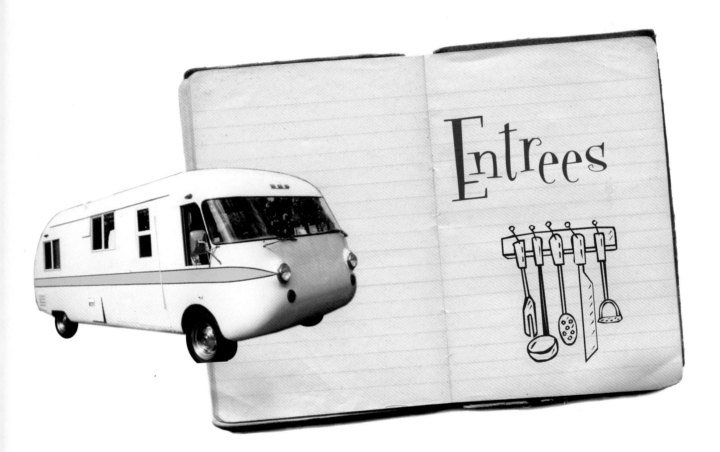

Entrees

Lola Miller, Fernley, Nevada

We have been RVing since 2001. We have a 33-foot 5th wheel. We decided to go RVing after my husband, Tom, retired from the City of Las Vegas Parks Department. We sold our home in Las Vegas and bought one in Grants Pass, Ore. There we met a couple who told us about RVing full time. So we sold everything and bought a 36-foot diesel pusher we call Big Bertha. She was an oldie but goodie. We have been going ever since, stopping for a little while here and there. We worked at some of the national parks the last couple of years; what a wonderful experience. We have been members of Good Sam Club for many years. We are in Fernley, Nevada, for awhile because we sold our 5th wheel and are now looking for a new home. We will purchase another smaller motor home after we buy our house. We could never give up RVing completely. It's a great way to travel!

BAKED ZITI WITH ITALIAN SAUSAGE & GROUND BEEF

Ingredients

1 jar (32 oz.) spaghetti sauce
1 jar (16 oz.) ricotta cheese
1 lb. shredded mozzarella cheese
2 Italian sausages
½ lb. ground beef
1 lb. ziti pasta

Instructions

Brown the beef and sausage (take out of casing), then add the spaghetti sauce. In the meantime, cook your pasta al dente. After pasta is cooked, drain and mix with ricotta cheese. Spoon sauce in a 9x12 pan (just a bottom layer of sauce), then add a layer of pasta, mozzarella, and a little sauce. Repeat until done. Sprinkle the top with mozzarella and parmesan cheese. Cover and bake in oven for 35 minutes at 350 degrees. Remove the cover and bake for 10 more minutes. Let set for 10 minutes; cut in squares and enjoy. May be topped with more sauce. Serve with garlic bread.

BERNI & BRIAR'S TORTILLA SCRAMBLE

Ingredients

1 dozen corn tortillas
1 dozen eggs
pinch of salt
pinch of pepper (to your liking)
pinch of garlic powder (optional)
pinch of onion powder
¼ C. cooking oil
salsa or ketchup

Instructions

Cut corn tortillas into bite-size squares. Place oil in frying pan on stove top or over campfire, or use an electric skillet, and heat with medium heat. Place cut tortilla pieces into hot oil and fry until desired crispiness, stir constantly to brown both sides of tortilla pieces. Place eggs in a bowl with salt, pepper, garlic powder, and onion powder; mix with whisk until thoroughly blended. After tortillas have crisped, pour egg mixture over tortillas and cook until eggs are done, constantly flipping and stirring for even cooking. Place in bowl and serve with salsa or ketchup. This recipe can be modified to your liking; you can add real onions, bacon pieces, sausage, bell pepper, red chili, or jalapenos. The kids like it just as the recipe states with ketchup; adults love it with salsa. It's so cheap and easy and fills you up. Cleanup is a breeze. This is a great recipe for camping.

RV Interior Designer

Betty Orr of Orr and Orr in Illinois was the first female interior designer in the trailer industry. She also was the first female president of a national association in the RV industry.

Berni and Briar Estes, Selma, Calif.

Our family has been RVing for several years. My mom and dad take us in their 5th wheel; we bring our cousins and have a great time. My mom lets me cook this recipe because it is easy, and it's the only thing my dad has ever cooked on the stove. Dad is definitely not the cook of the family, but can do a great BBQ. We are members of the Good Sam Club and my parents belong to the Tequila In Your Eye Club, which consists of several of their friends and my Nina Diana, Nino Scott, and Rachel, who are the diehard RVers in our club. I love to camp; we ride bikes and play, play, play and we get to take our dog Ty with us too. It's great being with my parents and friends. Everyone should RV!

BREAKFAST HAMBURGER HELPER

Ingredients

1 box Hamburger Helper Cheesy Hashbrowns
1 lb. pork sausage
2 C. hot water
⅓ C. milk

Instructions

Brown the sausage and crumble as you cook it in the Dutch oven or skillet over campfire coals or gas cooker. Stir in the HOT water and potatoes from Hamburger Helper package. Heat to boiling over high heat, stirring constantly until well mixed. No need to use margarine as instructed on box directions when using sausage. Reduce heat to medium-high; press potatoes and sausage evenly in bottom of pan or skillet. Cook uncovered for 5-7 minutes until liquid is absorbed and most of the bottom is browned. Meanwhile, stir milk and topping mix in a small bowl for 30 seconds and set aside. Cut the potatoes and sausage into small sections with the edge of a turner, slide turner under each section and turn over (mixture will not hold together completely). Press firmly; cook about 2-3 minutes until most of the bottom is brown. Remove from heat; pour topping over mixture in pan or skillet. Serve with choice of fried or scrambled eggs for an awesome campfire breakfast.

Sandi Hansen, Logan, Utah

My husband and I have been full-time RVers for 3 years now; we travel and are Workampers in RV parks and campgrounds working for FHU site plus wages as we are not retired yet (though we consider ourselves semi-retired). We live in a Carriage Carri-Lite 5th wheel with 5 slides. We belong to Workamper News as that is how we learn of and apply for the various job openings seasonally. We love this RV Workamper lifestyle for all the places we get to visit and the wonderful people we meet and work with along our journey.

BREAKFAST SAUSAGE WEDGES

Ingredients

1 package (12 oz.) pork sausage
1 unbaked deep-dish pastry pie shell (9 inch)
2 C. shredded cheddar cheese
3 eggs
1 C. salsa
sour cream, if desired

Instructions

Heat oven to 350 degrees. Crumble sausage and brown; drain. Sprinkle sausage over bottom of pie shell. Sprinkle sausage with cheese. In small bowl, beat eggs and blend in salsa. Pour egg mixture over cheese and sausage. Bake 25 to 35 minutes or until knife inserted in center comes out clean. Serve with sour cream and additional salsa, if desired.

Debbie Gleaves, Lawton, Okla.

BREAKFAST DISH

Ingredients
¼ C. melted butter
1 C. fine cracker crumbs
2 C. thinly sliced onion
2 T. butter
2 eggs
¾ C. milk
¾ t. salt
grated cheddar cheese

Instructions
Combine ¼ C. butter and cracker crumbs in a 9-inch pie pan. Sauté onion in 2 T. butter. Place in crumb shell. Top with eggs that are beaten with the milk and salt. Sprinkle desired amounts of cheese and bake in oven at 350 degrees for 30 minutes. Delicious with cooked bacon or sausage crumbled in.

Cassie, Somerville, Texas

We currently own a 33-foot travel trailer that we just purchased this year. My husband and I have two children, and we love taking the RV out on the weekend. We are making great memories as a family.

CALIFORNIA TACOS

Ingredients

1 lb. hamburger
1 C. chopped onion
1 clove garlic, minced
1 can tomato soup
1 can (6 oz.) tomato paste
2 ½ C. water
1 T. butter
⅔ C. Minute Rice (uncooked)
1 t. chili powder
1 t. cumin
2 t. sugar
1 ½ t. salt
⅓ t. pepper
dash of Tabasco
bag of regular flavor Doritos

Instructions

Brown hamburger and onions together; drain. Then add rest of ingredients except Doritos. Simmer for 30 minutes. Poke a small hole in the bag of Doritos and crunch them until they are bite size. To serve, place some crushed Doritos on a plate then top with the meat mixture and simply add your favorite toppings. Serves 4-6. Topping suggestions include shredded lettuce, diced fresh tomatoes, cubed avocado, black olives, grated cheddar cheese or pepper jack cheese, and, of course, salsa and sour cream. For a fun taco party, invite guests and ask them to bring their favorite topping for tacos. Add drinks and a dessert and you're good to go.

Queenie Malcolm, Charlotte, N.C.

We have been getting ready for a year and are now looking to purchase our Class A motor home. This has been a dream of ours forever. Our children are grown and it is now our turn. We are so excited about our new adventure.

CORN DOG TWIST

Ingredients

8 wooden sticks
8 wieners
1 can (11.5 oz) Pillsbury refrigerated
  cornbread twists
1 T. margarine or butter, melted
1 T. grated parmesan cheese

Instructions

Pre-heat oven to 375 degrees. Securely insert a wooden stick into end of each wiener. Unroll dough into one long sheet. Seal crosswise center perforations. Separate dough into 8 long strips (2 cornbread twists each). Wrap each strip around a wiener; place on ungreased cookie sheet with ends of dough tucked under wiener. Brush each with margarine. Sprinkle with cheese if desired. Bake for 12-16 minutes or until light golden brown. Serve immediately. You can put on coat hanger wire to cook over campfire, if desired.

Becky, Milano, Texas

I have been avid RVer since I was a little girl. I would love going on trips with my dad and older sister. I have great family memories of that special time in my life.

CREAM OF MUSHROOM MEATLOAF

Ingredients

1 ½ lb. ground beef or turkey
1 T. Worcestershire sauce
1 T. Liquid Smoke
salt and pepper to taste
1 can cream mushroom soup

Instructions

Mix first 4 ingredients together and only ½ can of soup; put in a spray oiled pan. (I use a bundt cake pan because the center does not cook the same in a microwave.) Microwave 15 minutes on medium-high level. Use a spoon to take any fat off the top; spread the other ½ can of soup. Put into the microwave for 2 minutes on high power.

Tina Praesel, Orange, Texas

 I am new to RVing but already love the freedom and adventure!

DROP THE HANDKERCHIEF

This is a great game for small children and is an early version of today's Duck, Duck, Goose game. Form a circle with players holding hands and one child who is "it" outside the circle. The child carries a large white handkerchief around the outside of the circle as the group chants, "A tisket, a tasket, a red and yellow basket. I wrote a letter to my fellow and on the way I dropped it." At that moment, the child drops the hanky on the ground behind one of the children in the circle. That child then chases the person around the circle, hoping to tag him before he slides into the vacant spot. If tagged, the person who was "it" continues. If not, the person chasing him becomes "it," and the song starts again.

DIPPING BATTER

Ingredients

1 C. sifted flour
½ t. salt
1 t. baking powder
1 egg, slightly beaten
¼ C. corn oil
1 C. milk

Instructions

Sift flour, salt, baking powder. Mix egg, corn oil, milk. Add to dry ingredients; beat with whisk until smooth. Dry food with paper towel; dust with flour mixture. Using tongs, dip food into the batter, then into hot oil (375 degrees). Fry until golden brown. Drain, season, and serve. For the cornmeal batter version follow the above recipe but use ¼ C. cornmeal and ¾ C. flour. Deep frying tips include using either a frying kettle or skillet for frying. Kettle or skillet should not be more than ⅓ full, but oil should be at least 1 inch deep. Add foods to hot oil slowly. Do not crowd kettle/skillet. You can save oil for another day. Cool; strain into a dry container, cover and store in refrigerator. Add a little fresh oil for next frying.

Virginia Praesel, Rockdale, Texas

HOBO PIZZA PIE

Ingredients

2 slices bread
2 t. butter
1 T. pizza sauce
¼ C. mozzarella cheese
1 Hobo Pie maker (sold at Walmart for $10)
Optional:
  pepperoni
  onions
  green peppers
  ham
  hamburger
  black olives
  pineapple
  sausage
  mushrooms

Instructions

Butter bread on one side (just like making a toasted cheese sandwich). Put the bread in the Hobo Pie maker with the buttered sides touching the metal. Fill with your favorite pizza toppings. Cook over the campfire. Keep an eye on it though, as they seem to cook quickly. They will look like toasted cheese sandwiches when done, but taste like wonderful, delicious pizza!

Misty Gustafson, Wooster, Ohio

We have been camping for many years. Right now, we are in a 5th wheel camper. We love the way it tows, almost like it's not behind us. We have been Workamper News members for a year now. Within that year, we started our Workamper job. It has been a great experience for us, something I would recommend to everyone.

HOT SANDWICHES

Ingredients

1 package frozen yeast rolls that come in an aluminum round pan, thawed
sliced lunch meat (we use chicken or turkey)
cheese slices (we use Swiss or provolone)
1 T. onion flakes (I sometimes use real onions and may also throw in some jalapenos)
1 stick melted butter
1 t. prepared mustard
1 t. Worcestershire sauce
1 T. poppy seeds (we sometimes delete this ingredient)

Instructions

Take the thawed rolls out of the aluminum pan and cut in half. I find cutting the rolls while they are still frozen makes them easier to cut in half. Put the bottom half back in the aluminum pan and then layer with cheese and meat and add the onions and jalapenos (if you are using them). In a small bowl melt the butter and add the other ingredients and mix. Pour half of the mixture over the cheese and meat. Put the top half of the rolls on top of the meat and pour the other half of the mixture on the top. Put the aluminum pan in a 10-inch Dutch oven. Put in the coals with coals on top to create a 350 degree oven (8 coals on bottom and 10 on top). Cook 45 minutes–until rolls are cooked and not doughy.

Jan Powell, Bolivar, Mo.

We have been full-time RVing since October 2009. We have a Hitchhiker 5th wheel with a one-ton dually. We belong to Escapees, Good Sam Club, and Workamper News. We also use Passport America, Club USA, and KOA as we travel.

ITALIAN HAM & CHEESE PIE

Ingredients

1 package Pillsbury pie crust (contains 2 crusts)
¼ C. each, cut into ¼-½ inch squares:
  ham, salami, pepperoni, Swiss cheese, mozzarella
¼ C. grated parmesan cheese
6 eggs, beaten
2 T. coarse ground black pepper

Instructions

Pre-heat convection oven to 350 degrees. Place one of the pie crusts into a pie pan. Mix all ingredients together in a bowl. Mixture should be soupy. Pour mixture into pie crust and cover with remaining crust. Cut slits in top crust. Bake for 30-40 minutes, depending on oven. Test for doneness by inserting skewer or knife tip into pie, which should come out clean if done. This delicious pie can be eaten hot or cold. It can be frozen for up to 30 days, but freezing does alter the texture of the pie somewhat. To freeze, wrap in clear wrap and then aluminum foil. Enjoy!

Mary T. Sandstrom, San Francisco, Calif.

We've been RVing for 3 years and love it. We recently took a 9-month trek from California to New York and back. We travel in a Class C Itasca Cambria and tow a Smart4Two car. We belong to the Good Sam Club, Escapees, WIT, FMCA, Coast-to-Coast, Camp Club USA, Camping World, KOA, Passport America, and Flying J. Since we are new to RVing, we're still testing the waters with these various clubs. So far, we haven't been disappointed with any of them, and actually used most of them on our cross-country trip. It was awesome!

JUGGERNAUTS HEALTHY MEATLOAF

Ingredients

1 lb. ground chicken
½ lb. ground pork
1 lb. ground lamb
1 ½ C. coarse oatmeal
3-4 cloves fresh minced garlic
1 egg
¼ C. ketchup
3 T. hot sauce
1 C. finely chopped onion
½ C. finely chopped green or red bell pepper
¼ C. raisins
¼ C. chopped carrots
1 T. curry
1 T. oregano
1 T. rosemary

Instructions

Pre-heat oven to 425 degrees. Mix all ingredients and form into one or two separate meatloaves. Make certain free-form is fairly solid and doesn't sag, or place in a bread form or similar pan. Add a few light cross cuts across tops of loaves and pour a bit of ketchup over them. Bake for 45 minutes. Lower oven to 300 degrees and bake an additional 30 minutes. Remove and tilt forms so any excess oil will drain until cool. Serve with a side of mashed sweet potatoes, greens, and a small salad.

Bob DeSanti, Grass Valley, Calif.

We have RVed full time since 1999. We tow our 33-foot three-slide Holiday Rambler 5th wheel with a 400 HP Volvo Semi registered as a motor home. After an 8-year absence, we have rejoined the Escapees Club and Workamper News.

LOW-FAT SPAGHETTI & MEAT SAUCE

Instructions

Brown the ground meat in a pan on the stove top and rinse in very hot water until all the fat is rinsed out. Add all ingredients except spaghetti and Italian seasoning. To measure the water, I just fill the tomato can 2 times if boiling down or 1 if cooking fast. Cook time is 15 minutes. The fast way is to simmer these all together. After 5 minutes of simmering, add the amount of spaghetti your family normally cooks, then add the Italian seasoning in the last 5 minutes of cooking. If you choose to cook spaghetti alone, use 1 can of water in the sauce; but if you cook spaghetti in the sauce, use 2 cans of water. The slower way is to simmer a long time, watching until the sauce looks the right consistency. Boil the spaghetti separately so you can control how much spaghetti you eat and add sauce on top. If you add a small amount of margarine to spaghetti then the spaghetti will not stick to itself. Serve with garlic toast and a salad. Note: You can use a 15 oz. can of diced tomatoes if you cook it for a long time on simmer. You can use low fat cream of mushroom soup to change it a little.

Ingredients

whole wheat spaghetti
1-1 ½ lbs. ground meat
salt and pepper to taste
1 T. Worcestershire sauce
½ T. Liquid Smoke
1 can (15 oz.) tomato sauce
1 small can mushrooms
1 t. Italian seasoning
water

Tina Praesel, Orange, Texas

RVIA's Beginnings

Paul Abel contributed greatly to the RVI in its early years, known now as the Recreation Vehicle Industry Association.

MAC & CHEESE, PINTOS, & CORNBREAD

Ingredients

1 box Kraft macaroni and cheese dinner
1 can of pinto beans
   margarine or butter, as needed
1 package of cornbread mix

Instructions

Prepare macaroni and cheese according to directions. Warm the pinto beans to boiling and then simmer. Prepare cornbread according to directions. You will then spoon cornbread into a frying pan that has margarine melted in it. You will be making cornbread pancakes, as my children called them. Flip when brown and cook on opposite side. Place on paper towels. This is a good southern meal when cool outside. This is also one of our favorites to fix when we camp.

Gail W. Yates, Pensacola, Fla.

We have been tenting for more than 33 years. We purchased our first RV in 1984. We now own a 2005 Winnebago Adventurer and tow a 2006 Subaru Forester. We are lifetime members of the Good Sam Club.

Lori Stewart, Columbus, Ohio

My husband and I have been RVing since 2000. We started with a 25-foot travel trailer, moved up to a 35-foot 5th wheel, and currently have a 37-foot Bounder motor home. I am a member and site moderator on iRV2.com, a social website which supports the thoughtful exchange of knowledge, values, and experience among RV enthusiasts.

MEATBALLS IN MUSHROOM GRAVY

Ingredients

Meatballs:
- 1 lb. ground chuck
- ¼ lb. ground veal
- ¼ lb. ground pork
- ¼ lb. mild sausage
- 1 egg
- 2 T. dried parsley
- ½ C. grated parmesan cheese
- 1 ½ t. salt
- ¼ t. pepper
- 1 ½ C. bread crumbs

Gravy:
- 1 can (4 oz.) mushrooms, drained
- 1 can (10.75 oz.) cream of mushroom soup
- 1 small onion, chopped
- 1 C. sour cream
- ⅓ C. flour
- ½ T. Worchestershire sauce
- ¼ C. dry sherry
- 1 t. paprika

Instructions

Combine all gravy ingredients in crock pot and stir until blended. Mix together all meatball ingredients and shape into meatballs. Brown in skillet. Add meatballs to gravy mixture in crock pot. Cover and cook on low 7-9 hours or on high 3-4 hours. Serve over noodles, rice, or mashed potatoes. Makes 4-6 servings. Note: You may substitute a 16 oz. bag of frozen meatballs for quicker prep time.

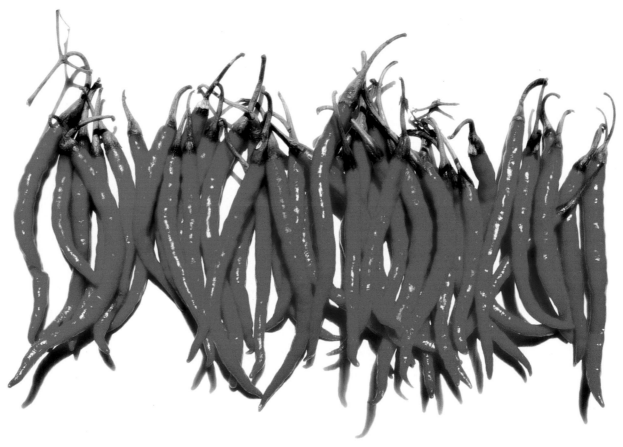

Greg Gerber, Sun City, Ariz.

Greg Gerber is the editor of *RV Daily Report* and the former editor of *RV Trade Digest* and *RV Industry News*. He and his family purchased a pop-up camper in 2002, which was sold when his daughters got "too old" to go camping. He is looking forward to the day he'll get another RV to travel the country for work and pleasure. This recipe was developed by Greg and his mentor in Big Brothers, David Mond (with Big Brothers and Big Sisters), in the mid-1970s.

METHANE MADNESS: A SWEET CHILI

Ingredients

2 lbs. ground beef
1 lb. bacon
1 large yellow onion
2 green peppers
2 cans chili beans
2 cans kidney beans
2 cans Great Northern white beans
1 C. brown sugar
1 jar (12 oz.) Open Pit barbecue sauce
1 T. vinegar
Tabasco sauce

Instructions

Brown ground beef, drain grease, and place beef in large mixing bowl. Cut bacon into 1-inch strips; cook, drain grease, and add bacon strips to mixing bowl. Sauté onions and green peppers in skillet; place in bowl. Empty beans into bowl without draining. Add brown sugar, barbecue sauce, vinegar, and 8 shots of Tabasco sauce. Mix well. Place in large crock pot and cook for 3-4 hours until beans are tender.
Some people like to add shredded cheddar cheese, sour cream, or salsa/hot sauce–serve on the side. Feeds 6-8. Due to heavy bean content, meal is best consumed outdoors!

MEXICAN LASAGNA

Ingredients

1 ½ lb. lean ground beef
1 package taco seasoning (El Paso brand)
1 can Ro★Tel Mexican blend
2 packages corn tortillas
2 C. small curd cottage cheese (large container)
1 egg
1 C. grated hot pepper jack cheese
dash salt
2 T. black pepper
Topping:
  1 C. chopped lettuce
  1 C. chopped tomatoes
  1 C. chopped onions
  1 small can sliced black olives
  1 C. chopped green olives
  1 jar salsa (mild/medium/hot)
sour cream
  1 C. grated mild cheddar cheese

Instructions

Pre-heat oven to 350 degrees. Brown ground beef in skillet and drain off fat; add taco seasoning pack and RoTel to browned beef and cook at a simmer for 10 minutes. Spray 13x9 baking dish with Pam. Layer bottom of dish with corn tortillas. Mix cottage cheese, egg, salt, pepper, and hot pepper jack cheese together in medium bowl. Spread ground beef mixture on top of tortillas, then put another layer of corn tortillas on top of the ground beef, then spread the cottage cheese mixture on top of the tortillas very carefully. Be sure to cover all the tortillas with the mixture. Bake for 30 minutes uncovered. Add the topping ingredients as desired. Great with side dish of refried beans and chips. Enjoy!

Rich and Kitty Grenier, Mims, Fla.

We have been Workampers and full timing for 3 great years, enjoying every minute. We own a 38-foot KZ Escalade 5th wheel, which we pull with our 350 Ford dually. We are members of the Good Sam Club.

MEXICAN PANCAKES

Ingredients

1 C. cornmeal
1 C. boiling water
1 C. milk
½ C. salad oil
1 egg
1 C. Bisquick
1 pinch salt
½ t. cumin
½ t. chili powder
2 t. baking powder
8 oz. corn, fresh or canned
½ C. olives, sliced or minced
Condiments (any or all):
   shredded cheese, chopped green onions,
   chopped tomatoes, sour cream, taco sauce, salsa

Instructions

Put cornmeal in a bowl and pour boiling water over it. Let cool for 10 minutes. Add milk, salad oil, and well-beaten egg. Mix well. Add Bisquick, salt, cumin, chili powder, and baking powder. Beat until smooth. Add corn and olives. Pre-heat griddle/skillet. Spoon on batter to desired size. Cook until bubbles appear. Turn over and continue cooking until done. When serving, pass bowls of any condiments. Top with sour cream, salsa, and/or taco sauce.

Frank Rowley, Napa, Calif.

I have been RVing full time for 4 years and camp host in the Arizona area. I own a 5th wheel rig.

tech tip

Please use only a certi-
fied leak detector or an
electronic propane detec-
tor to find leaks in a propane system. Open flames
are NOT the safe way to
find a leak.

OVEN-FRIED CHICKEN

Ingredients

1 T. margarine or butter
⅔ C. Bisquick baking mix
2 ⅓ to 3 ½ lb. chicken, cut up
1 ½ t. paprika
1 ¼ t. salt
¼ t. pepper

Instructions

Pre-heat oven to 425 degrees. Melt margarine in a 13x9 pan in oven. Mix baking mix, paprika, salt, and pepper; coat chicken. Place skin side down in pan. Bake 35 minutes, then turn. Cook until done, approximately 15 minutes.

Stephanie, Mesquite, Texas

PEPPERED SHRIMP

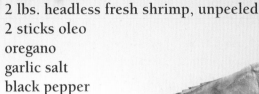

Ingredients

2 lbs. headless fresh shrimp, unpeeled
2 sticks oleo
oregano
garlic salt
black pepper

Instructions

Place single layer of shrimp in large baking dish. Sprinkle lightly with oregano, garlic salt, and pepper. Cover with sliced margarine. Cover with foil and bake in 400 degree oven for 15 minutes. (Can also be cooked in a pan over a campfire.) Turn with spatula, add more black pepper, and cook another 15 minutes. Stir and serve. Black pepper flavor without the heat.

Chris, Somerville, Texas

I have had an RV of some kind for many years. Currently, I am restoring a teardrop travel trailer from the 1950s. I love the old retro styles.

POTATO CASSEROLE

Ingredients

1 package (2 lbs.) Ore-Ida frozen hash browns, thawed
½ C. onion, chopped
2 C. grated cheese
1 stick of margarine, melted
1 can cream of mushroom soup
1 carton (16 oz.) sour cream
2 C. cornflakes
salt and pepper to taste

Instructions

Mix all ingredients except butter. Spread into a lightly greased casserole dish. Crush cornflakes with melted butter, then pour over potato mixture. Bake at 350 degrees for 45 minutes.

Rona Locke, Georgetown, Texas

I have been camping since I was young (35 years ago). I would go on summer trips with my grandparents who traveled in a pop-up and in later years, a travel trailer then motor home. I have fond memories of spending special quality time with them while RVing.

QUICK & EASY CHICKEN CRESCENTS

Ingredients

1 ½-2 C. diced, cooked chicken (or 1-2 large cans of boned chicken)
4 oz. cream cheese (regular or light)
3 t. poultry seasoning
1 t. dill weed
salt and pepper to taste
1 can refrigerated crescent rolls
1 can cream of chicken soup (optional)

Instructions

Mix cream cheese, chicken, and seasonings together. Unroll crescent rolls and separate into individual triangles. Spoon out and spread chicken mixture onto crescent rolls and roll up as you would a crescent roll. Bake in oven or toaster oven at 350 degrees until rolls are done (approximately 10 minutes) and browned slightly on top. Serve these with a salad or pop them into bags and take them on a hike or your favorite adventure. They're great hot or cold! You can also heat cream of chicken soup and serve over rolls.

Carla Brownfield, Round Rock, Texas

My husband and I (native Texans) began RVing full time in 2005 in a 32-foot 5th wheel and have been Workampers as we traveled across the U.S. for 3 years. We thoroughly enjoyed our work and stays in Maine, Missouri, Texas, and California as well as other adventures coast to coast. The friends we made along the way are still among our best friends. Being members of Good Sam Club, Passport America, and KOA made our journey even more enjoyable and affordable. Being without an RV since the summer of 2008, we are now anxiously searching for our next 5th wheel so we can begin full timing again this year. There's nothing like being on the road, meeting new people, and sharing new experiences with other RVers. We'll be on the road again before you know it!

REUBEN SANDWICHES

Trailer Capital

In the late 1940s, Elkhart, Ind., became known as the Trailer Capital of the World.

Ingredients

rye bread
sauerkraut
sliced Swiss cheese
canned corned beef
thousand island dressing
margarine

Instructions

Make a sandwich with a slice of Swiss cheese on the rye bread, place a slice or two of corned beef on the cheese, and layer with sauerkraut and thousand island dressing. Butter the outsides of the bread and cook in electric skillet or on stove top like you would a toasted cheese sandwich. Eat hot. We also use cast iron pie holders over a campfire to heat the sandwiches.

Jan Powell, Bolivar, Mo.

We have been full-time RVers since October 2009. We belong to Escapees, Workamper News, and Good Sam Club. We own a HitchHiker 5th wheel pulled by a one-ton dually truck.

SAUSAGE & VEGGIE BAKE

Ingredients

1 or 2 sausages
1 stalk of broccoli
1 stalk of cauliflower
1 carrot
aluminum foil

Instructions

Place all ingredients onto a piece of foil and wrap it up tightly. Leave two handles on the ends to pick it up with. Place in coals of campfire and leave for 5-10 minutes until everything is cooked.

Yvonne Baker, College Station, Texas

When I was a child, my siblings and I would go RVing with my grandparents. As adults, my sister and I would take our families together on RVing trips while our children were young. That was many years ago. Now our children are doing the same thing with their children. Our family has had a wonderful history with RVing. I'm sure it will continue all because of the love of RVing our grandparents had all those years ago.

RV Games

Freeze Tag

When the weather is hot and youngsters are bored, the very thought of Freeze Tag can cool things off a bit. Choose someone to be "it." Players scatter while the person who is "it" closes his/her eyes and counts to 10. The person who is "it" then tries to catch other players by tagging them. When tagged, that person "freezes" and cannot move unless another unfrozen player tags them and unfreezes them. Once all players are "frozen," the first one caught becomes "it," and the game begins again.

SPAM PINEAPPLE DELIGHT

Ingredients

1 can Spam Lite
1 large can of pineapple chunks in pineapple juice
2 C. prepared rice
soy sauce
salt and pepper

Instructions

Cut up Spam into cubes approximately same size as pineapple chunks. Sauté the Spam until edges are brown. Add whole can of pineapple with the juice. Use spatula to stir and deglaze the pan of the good bits of Spam that may have stuck to the pan. Add soy sauce, salt, and pepper to taste. Simmer for 15 minutes. Place cooked rice on plate and spoon Spam pineapple mixture over rice. Enjoy!

Debbie Slone, Ft. Meyers, Fla.

We have been RVing for 15 years and have been full-timers for 3 ½ years. We live in a Monaco Class A motor home with our chocolate lab. We love the lifestyle and traveling from campground to campground to live and work. We enjoy meeting new friends and look forward to traveling to see family and friends between jobs.

TEXAS TRAVELERS STEW

Ingredients

2 lbs. hamburger meat (80/20 is best)
1 package Lipton soup mix
2 medium potatoes, sliced
1 onion, sliced
1 bell pepper, seeded and sliced
1 small can corn, drained
1 small can green beans, drained
1 small can peas, drained
1 small can carrots, drained
your choice of seasoning
butter
heavy duty foil

Instructions

This recipe is great for the whole family to assemble together; the kids love it. Begin by forming 8-12 inch square sheets of foil, then mix the hamburger meat with the onion soup mix and form into quarter-pound patties and set on the foil. Start stacking on your veggies, then put a pat of butter on top and season to taste. Now close up each foil pocket, being very careful to leave plenty of room for the steam to form during cooking. Place on campfire grill for 30-45 minutes or in RV oven at 400 degrees for about 30 minutes. Cleanup is a breeze too. Just serve in foil pocket and throw away when you're finished. CAUTION: When opening hot pocket, beware of steam!

Debi and Eddie Hurlburt, Conroe, Texas

We have been RVing about 12 years now. Our best trip so far was in October of 2001, up the East Coast from Texas to Maine pulling a 25–foot travel trailer. Breathtaking tree colors were changing to the fall bliss. In Georgia, we saw turtle crossings; in Virginia, we saw the first English settlement in Jamestown; in Maine, we ate lobster and I saw my first chipmunk. In Washington, D.C., they found anthrax in the mail, and in Hershey, Pa., we went on a chocolate tour. In Cumberland Gap, Tenn., we saw runaway lanes for large trucks and RVs that can't slow down due to steep declines. In Hurricane Mills, Tenn., we visited Loretta Lynn's house. (Her house is haunted by Civil War slaves!) We gambled at the casinos in Mississippi. There is so much more to tell and so little space. We have never met a stranger at any of the Good Sam Clubs (members since 2000) or KOA sites at which we stayed. We can't wait until retirement in 2011 to go RVing north and west, this time in our 32–foot Allegro motor home.

Desserts

64554

5-MINUTE CHOCOLATE MUG CAKE

Ingredients

4 T. flour
4 T. sugar
2 T. cocoa
1 egg
3 T. milk
3 T. oil
3 T. chocolate chips (optional)
small splash of vanilla extract
1 large coffee mug (microwave safe)

Instructions

Add dry ingredients to mug and mix well. Add egg and mix thoroughly. Pour in the milk and oil; mix well. Add chocolate chips (if using) and vanilla extract; mix again. Put mug in microwave and cook for 3 minutes at 1000 watts. The cake will rise over the top of the mug, but don't be alarmed! Allow to cool a little, and tip out onto a plate if desired. (This can serve two if you want to feel slightly more virtuous.) And why is this most dangerous cake recipe in the world? Because now we are only 5 minutes away from chocolate cake at any time of the day or night!

Harriet Miller, Fort Wayne, Ind.

Since 2007, I have been a member of RVing Women (Ohio River Valley and Great Lakes Chapters) and the owner of a 1996 Minnie Winnie.

APPLE DUMPLINGS

Ingredients

2 Granny Smith apples, peeled and cut into 8 wedges for each apple (16 total wedges)
2 cans refrigerator biscuits
1 C. sugar
1 stick softened butter
1 t. cinnamon
1 t. vanilla
1 can (12 oz.) Mountain Dew (can be diet)

Instructions

Flatten a biscuit and wrap a slice of apple in it. (Try to cover the apple but don't worry if there's apple not quite covered with biscuit dough.) Put into 9x13 pan. Do all the apples this way and place side by side into pan. In small bowl, mix sugar, softened butter, cinnamon, and vanilla together and spoon over apples and biscuits. Pour Mountain Dew over top. Bake 350 degrees for 45 minutes. (For a 10-inch Dutch oven, cut the recipe in half and put ingredients in a round cake pan in your Dutch oven. Bake with 8 coals on bottom and 10 coals on top for about 45 minutes to 1 hour.) Serve warm or cold. Warm with ice cream topping is yummy!

Jan Powell, Bolivar, Mo.

The house is gone, and we have been RVing full time since October 2009. We own a HitchHiker 5th wheel and belong to Escapees, Good Sam Club, and Workamper News. We use Passport America, Camp Club USA, and KOA. We are currently sitting in Northern Idaho working for the Corps of Engineers after wintering in Hondo, Texas, with friends we met at the Escapades Albuquerque Balloon Fiesta HOP. We have been camping for the past 30 years, but love the full-time lifestyle after careers in professional fields.

APPLE ENCHILADAS

Ingredients

1 can apple pie filling
6 flour tortillas
1 t. cinnamon
⅓ C. stick margarine
½ C. brown sugar
½ C. water

Instructions

Spoon fruit filling evenly down the center of the tortillas. Sprinkle evenly with cinnamon. Roll up and place face down in a greased dish. In a separate pan, mix the brown sugar and water; bring to a boil. Reduce heat and simmer for 3 minutes. Pour over the enchiladas. Bake in oven for 30 minutes at 350 degrees. Serve warm with vanilla ice cream (optional).

Debbie Statsman, Ardmore, Okla.

 We have been full timing for 2 years. We started in a small travel trailer and have graduated to a cozy 5'er.

BETTY'S CHERRY COBBLER

Ingredients

2 cans (21 oz.) cherry pie filling
1 package yellow cake mix, dry
¼ C. softened butter
½ C. pecans, chopped

Instructions

Pour pie filling into the crock pot or slow cooker. In bowl, place dry cake mix and softened butter. Mix until crumbly. Sprinkle over pie filling then top with pecans. Place a sheet of paper towel under lid and cook on low for 3 to 4 hours. Serve warm. Recommended toppings: vanilla ice cream or whipped topping. Great for potlucks and absolutely terrific taste!

Joanne Molnar, Jacksonville, N.C.

We have both been RVing on family vacations since we were kids. Now we are living the dream. We have been full timing since 2008. We love the life. We are members of Workamper News and are working in Jacksonville, N.C.

CHEESE DANISH

Ingredients

1 package (8 oz.) cream cheese, softened at room temperature
⅓ C. Splenda
2 extra large egg yolks, room temperature
2 T. ricotta cheese
1 t. vanilla extract
¼ t. salt
1 T. grated lemon zest
2 sheets (1 box) puff pastry, defrosted
1 egg beaten with 1 T. water for egg wash
¼ C. Splenda
3 t. cinnamon

Instructions

Place cream cheese and sugar in a bowl of an electric mixer and cream together on low until smooth. Add egg yolks, ricotta, vanilla, salt, and lemon zest and mix until just combined. Unfold 1 sheet of puff pastry on a lightly floured board and roll it with a floured rolling pin until it's a 10x10-inch square. Cut the sheet into quarters. Brush the edges and the center cuts of the pastry with egg wash. Place a heaping tablespoon of cheese filling in the middle of the four squares. Take one corner and lay it over the filling and brush the corner with egg wash. Take the opposite corner and drape it over the corner with the egg wash. Place the squares on the cookie sheet and brush the tops with egg wash. Repeat with second sheet of puff pastry. Refrigerate the pastries for 15 minutes. Sprinkle the Danish with the Splenda/cinnamon mixture and put in oven. Bake for 10 minutes at 400 degrees. Turn the pan around and bake another 10 minutes or until puffed and brown.

Vickie Medley, The Woodlands, Texas

We have been avidly researching full-time RVing. As soon as the house sells, we will be buying a motor home that will become our permanent home. Our business is such that we can do it on the road and still travel. We're excited and can hardly wait to begin!

CHERRY DELIGHT

Ingredients

 1 box of cinnamon graham crackers
  (you will need 1.5 to 2 packages)
 8 T. or 1 stick butter or margarine
 1 can sweetened condensed milk
 ⅓ C. lemon juice
 1 envelope of Dream Whip
  (will also need ½ C. cold milk and ½ t. vanilla
  for preparation)
 2 cans of cherry pie filling
 1 9x13 baking pan or dish

Instructions

Melt butter or margarine. Crush your packages of cinnamon grahams to fine crumbs. Mix butter and crumbs. Pack into lightly greased baking dish to form your bottom crust. Refrigerate to cool. Prepare the Dream Whip according to directions on the package. Mix in the sweetened condensed milk and lemon juice. Pour this mixture over the crust. Cover this mixture with the cherry pie filling. Refrigerate. Enjoy!

Gail W. Yates, Pensacola, Fla.

CHOCOLATE PEANUT BUTTER COOKIES

Ingredients

12-16 oz. chocolate chips or sugar-free bars
Ritz-type crackers
smooth or crunchy peanut butter
wax paper
double boiler
tongs
spoon to stir

Instructions

Put water in one pan but not enough to float the second pan. Put chocolate in top pan so it does not boil. Do not boil the water; just keep it hot. Mix with spoon often, because it can look like it is not melting and then it will burn. Take the crackers and spread peanut butter on one and top with the other. Using the tongs, dip the crackers in chocolate and place on the wax paper to cool. Once cool, leave wax paper in between layers of cookies to keep separated when storing them. Leave them out but away from heat. Watch out, they go fast!

Tina Praesel, Orange, Texas

CRANBERRY SALAD DESSERT

Ingredients

1 package cranberries
40 grapes
3 C. miniature marshmallows
2 C. sugar
1 C. nuts, chopped
½ pint whipping cream

tech tip

Did you know that for every minute the refrigerator door is left open it will take the refrigerator 1 hour to recover?

Instructions

Chop cranberries in a food processor and set in bowl with sugar for 2 hours. Pit, slice, and add grapes. Add marshmallows and nuts. Whip cream and fold in. Refrigerate overnight.

Stephanie, Mesquite, Texas

DAUGTHER-IN-LAW'S CANDY DROPS

Ingredients

1 baked cake (any flavor)
¾ can grocery store icing (any flavor)
1 C. melted chocolate (any flavor)

Instructions

Bake cake. While the cake is warm, mix the icing into it which will make the cake gooey. Like making a meatball, roll into small balls. Dip into melted chocolate. Cool in refrigerator and serve.

Pat, W.Va.

I retired after 40 years of teaching, sold everything, and became a solo full-time RVer and work camper, which was all completely new to me. After 5 years, I am still having a great time. I've worked in Key Largo, Florida, where I learned to snorkel; in Colorado where I learned about horses; in Mission, Texas where I learned great Mexican traditions, and many other locations from coast to coast meeting great friends along the way. I love the fact that when you work a season, you really get to explore the area and take in all the local events.

DUMP CAKE

Ingredients

1 box yellow cake mix
2 sticks butter
1 can cherry pie filling
1 can blackberry pie filling
walnuts (optional)

Instructions

Using a glass 9x13 pan, layer the ingredients. First layer is the pie fillings. Cover them with the DRY cake mix. Melt butter and pour over the top. If you wish, sprinkle walnuts on top. Bake in the oven at 350 degrees for 1 hour or until browned and bubbly.

Elaine Shultz, Wickes, Ark.

We used to camp out in the back of our old truck (or the back of the big firewood truck my dad had for several years) when we collected firewood near Lindrith, New Mexico, back in the late 1960s to early 1970s. It was wild and beautiful. We had to watch for the mountain lions, but that made it even more exciting!

Tin Can Tourists

The Tin Can Tourists made up one of the earliest RV camping clubs in the 1920s and '30s. Driving in Tin Lizzies before roads were paved, the early RVers camped by the side of the road, heating tin cans of food on a gasoline stove.

EASIEST EVER FUDGE

Ingredients

2 bags Wilton chocolate disks (purchase at hobby or craft stores)
1 jar marshmallow crème
1 can sweetened condensed milk
1 C. chopped nuts, any kind (optional)
1 t. vanilla

Instructions

Melt chocolate in 1 minute increments in microwave until melted.
Stir in condensed milk and marshmallow crème. Reheat if necessary.
Stir in nuts and vanilla last. Work quickly and spread in 9x11 pan.
Let set in refrigerator and cut in desired sized squares. Enjoy!

Brenda S. Hill, Johnson City, Tenn.

My husband and I have been RVing since 1976. We have an Allegro Bus, 40-foot diesel pusher. We have been work camping now for the past 5 years and loving it. It allows us to meet folks from everywhere and make lifelong friends. We are not members of a club at the present time, as we are pretty much on our own with work camping. This recipe was a brainchild from when we were camping on the Natchez Trace and found piles of hickory nuts. I made this candy for campfire friends at the park we were in. It was the best candy I have made in a long time, enjoyed by all.

EASY DOUGHNUTS

Ingredients

"Grand's" type biscuits (not the layered ones)
sugar or powdered sugar (optional)
cinnamon (optional)

Instructions

Use a Dutch oven with bale handle over fire on a tripod. Separate the biscuits and break in half for easier cooking. Flatten or make hole–it looks like a real doughnut. Flip often to keep from overcooking and turn in powdered sugar or cinnamon and sugar or whatever you like on yours.

Jim, Watertown, Wis.

 I have been RVing for 25 years and own a class A motor home.

EASY PUMPKIN DESSERT DIP

Ingredients

1 package (8 oz.) cream cheese, softened
1 jar (7 oz.) marshmallow crème
½ C. canned pumpkin
¼ t. cinnamon
¼ t. nutmeg

Instructions

Mix all ingredients until blended; cover.
Refrigerate for at least one hour, then serve
with cookies or fresh fruit.

Pam, Caldwell, Texas

I am in my mid-50s and have been RVing since I was a child. Its was always a large family event. Reunions would
bring all the RVs and tents together for a great time.

FRUIT PIZZA

Ingredients

1 package (18 oz.) refrigerated sugar cookie dough
1 package (8 oz.) cream cheese, room temperature
⅓ C. sugar
½ t. vanilla extract or other flavoring (almond, orange, or lemon)
Fresh blueberries, banana slices, mandarin orange sections,
   seedless grapes, strawberry halves, kiwifruit (or any other)
½ C. orange, peach, or apricot preserves
1 T. water

Instructions

Pre-heat oven to 375 degrees. Line an ungreased 14-inch pizza pan with cookie dough cut into triangles, overlapping slightly. Bake 12 minutes or until light brown; remove from oven and cool on a wire rack. In a medium bowl, combine cream cheese, sugar, and vanilla extract or other flavoring; spread over cookie crust. Arrange fruit over cream cheese layer in any design you want (use your imagination). In a small saucepan over very low heat, make a glaze by heating preserves and water. Brush glaze over fruit, making sure to cover the fruit that will turn dark. Refrigerate until ready to serve. Note: This does not keep well, so plan on using it up. You may also use your own sugar cookie recipe in place of the refrigerated dough. This recipe was given a 5 star rating from an online recipe site. I love it! Fun for kids and adults alike!

Stephanie, Mesquite, Texas

GRAPE DESSERT

Ingredients

3 lbs. red or green seedless grapes
1 C. white sugar
8 oz. sour cream
8 oz. Philadelphia brand cream cheese
1 t. vanilla
Topping:
   1 C. light brown sugar
   ground nuts

Instructions

Wash and stem the grapes; dry well. Mix sugar, sour cream, cream cheese, and vanilla with electric mixer until well blended, then stir in grapes carefully. Pour in 9x12 dish. For the topping, mix ground nuts and brown sugar together; sprinkle over top. This dessert can also be used as a salad. Keeps well for 3-4 days.

Ann Griffey, Shelbyville, Ind.

HOBO PIES

Ingredients

2 slices of bread
2 T. pie filling (apple, blueberry, or cherry)
1 t. butter
1 Hobo Pie maker (sold at Walmart for around $10)

Instructions

Butter bread on one side (just like making a toasted cheese sandwich). Put the bread in the Hobo Pie maker with the buttered sides touching the metal. Fill with your favorite pie topping (as little or as much as you like). Cook over the campfire. Keep an eye on it though, as they seem to cook quickly. They will look like toasted cheese sandwiches when done, but taste like wonderful, delicious desserts!

Misty Gustafson, Wooster, Ohio

First Camping Vehicles

1910 is when the first camping vehicles were built for commercial sale. Known as auto campers and camping trailers a century ago, these vehicles became forerunners of today's modern motorhomes, travel trailers, folding camping trailers, and truck campers.

LEMON CHEESE POUND CAKE

Ingredients

1 box white cake mix
1 small can frozen lemonade
1 small carton sour cream
3 eggs
powdered sugar
3 oz. cream cheese

Instructions

Blend all ingredients together, except for powdered sugar,
and bake in oven in greased bundt pan at 350 degrees for 40
to 45 minutes. After cooling cake, dust with powdered sugar.

Pam, Caldwell, Texas

I am now in my mid-50s and have been RVing since I was a child. It was always a large family event. Reunions would
bring all the RVs and tents together for a great time.

LEMON POUND CAKE

Ingredients

1 box lemon cake mix
1 box lemon instant pudding
4 eggs
7 oz. lemon-lime drink
¾ C. oil

Instructions

Combine and beat until smooth. Pour into a bundt pan that has been greased and floured. Bake in oven at 350 degrees for 50 to 60 minutes.

tech tip

If shade drapes across any part of a solar panel, that row of cells loses its ability to produce power.

Sharon Lexington, Texas

My husband and I owned a 5th wheel for a few years, then sold it and recently purchased a motor home. We RV for a few months then go back home for a few months. We have enjoyed seeing the sights and traveling.

ORANGE SHELL CAKE

Ingredients

1 box (8 oz.) Jiffy yellow cake mix
6 large thick skin oranges
water
1 egg
heavy foil

Instructions

Slice 2 inches from the top of the oranges and save. Remove orange from shell, being careful not to damage shell. Prepare cake mix per instructions. Fill each orange shell half full of cake mix. Replace top and wrap in foil. Bake in campfire or on grill about 20 minutes, turning often. When the cakes are done, eat with a spoon or peel the orange and eat.

Pamela A. Praesel, Bryan, Texas

PEACH COBBLER

Ingredients

4 cans (15 oz.) sliced peaches in light syrup
1 box yellow cake mix
vanilla ice cream
charcoal briquettes

Instructions

Light the charcoal briquettes about 30-45 minutes before getting cobbler together. Drain the cans of peaches, reserving the juice. Mix the cake mix with the reserved peach juice. Put the sliced peaches in a small Dutch oven; pour the cake mixture over the peaches. Put lid on Dutch oven. Place Dutch oven over coals or on gas cooker and put briquette coals on top of Dutch oven lid (so the top gets cooked also). Cook on medium-low for about 35-45 minutes until top of cobbler is light brown and done. Serve warm with vanilla ice cream.

Sandi Hansen, Logan, Utah

My husband and I are semi-retired, living full time in our RV and Workamping in different areas of the western states. We love what we do and the people we meet and become special friends with. We live in a 37-foot 5th wheel with five slides. It's a Carriage Carri-Lite. We belong to Workamper News and get daily notifications of new job openings that we can apply to work for, usually on a seasonal basis.

PERSONAL PINEAPPLE UPSIDE DOWN CAKE

Ingredients

sliced pineapple (1 slice per person)
glazed donut, Krispy Kreme style (1 donut per person)
brown sugar (1 T. per person)
cherries (1 per person)

Instructions

Lay out a 6x6-inch piece of foil. Layer donut and pineapple; put cherry in donut hole and sprinkle with brown sugar. Wrap in foil and place in campfire coals for about 5 minutes.

Michelle Boykin, Oklahoma City, Okla.

 I have been camping with my family since I was born.

PIG PICKIN' CAKE

Ingredients

1 box (18.25 oz.) yellow cake mix
1 can (11 oz.) mandarin oranges, juices reserved
4 eggs
¼ C. vegetable oil
1 package (16 oz.) frozen whipped topping, thawed
1 can (15 oz.) crushed pineapple, drained
1 package (3.5 oz.) instant vanilla pudding mix

Instructions

Mix together cake mix, canned mandarin oranges with juice, eggs, and oil. Pour batter into 3 greased and floured 8-inch round pans. Layer will be thin. Bake in oven at 350 degrees for 25 to 30 minutes, or until cake tests as done. Cool layers on wire racks. Mix together whipped topping, drained pineapple, and instant pudding mix. Fill and frost the cooled cake. Refrigerate until ready to eat.

Subie, Redd, Texas

This is a recipe I used to make often when we were traveling in the RV. Rick and I have known about Steve Anderson, who now owns Workamper News, since his days at Adventureland in Iowa. We have worked for Steve; in fact, that is how we came to the Rio Grande Valley. We don't travel anymore, but still talk often about our travels and the folks we have met along the way.

PINA COLADA CAKE

Ingredients

1 box white cake mix, without pudding is better
1 can (15 oz.) cream of coconut
1 can (14 oz.) sweetened condensed milk
1 small container of Cool Whip
coconut, if desired

Instructions

Bake cake mix as directed. As it bakes, mix the cream of coconut and condensed milk together. Immediately when cake is done, poke holes all over the cake and slowly pour cream of coconut mixture over the top. Put covered cake in refrigerator and after it has cooled, spread Cool Whip over the top. You may sprinkle the Cool Whip with lightly browned coconut if you like.

Debbie Gleaves, Lawton, Okla.

PINEAPPLE SOUR CREAM PIE

Ingredients

1 small package vanilla instant pudding
1 container (16 oz.) sour cream
1 T. sugar (optional)
1 can (8 oz.) crushed pineapple, undrained
1 graham cracker pie shell

Instructions

Mix first 4 ingredients. Pour into pie shell and chill. Garnish, if desired, with whipped cream and fresh fruit (strawberries and kiwi, etc.).

Marilyn Brown, Portland, Ore.

I retired in 2006 and have been RVing ever since with my 2005 35-foot Winnebago Voyage with my Saturn in tow. My first trip was from Portland, Ore., to Orlando, Fla., and back, visiting friends and family along the way. I am a member of Workamper News and just finished an assignment at Palm Creek Golf & RV Resort in Casa Grande, Arizona. I'm on my way to Colorado, then back to Arizona for future Workamping. My favorite place to RV is the Oregon coast. I have been a member of Good Sam Club and Escapees since 2003. (I use Escapees' mail forwarding service.) This is the most incredible lifestyle, and I wouldn't trade it for anything. I have met some wonderful people and keep in touch with many of them and my family via email. The recipe I submitted takes about 5 minutes to make. I have shared it at many potlucks along my travels and it always get raves. Enjoy!

PINEAPPLE UPSIDE DOWN CAKE

Ingredients

1 box white cake mix
1 can crushed pineapple
1 C. brown sugar
butter for pan
aluminum foil
22 pieces charcoal
Dutch oven with feet

Instructions

Line Dutch oven with foil, then butter the inside of the foil. Put pineapple and juice in and spread evenly. Sprinkle brown sugar into pineapple. Mix cake per instructions and pour into the pan. Put lid on and place oven over 12 pieces of charcoal. Put 10 pieces of charcoal on top of oven. In 45 minutes test with toothpick. If done turn over onto a plate and remove foil. Cut and serve.

Dale Noel, Howell, Mich.

I've been camping since I was a child, RVing with my family since 1976 using pop-ups, Class C and A, and presently have a 322FKS Jayco Eagle. We camp with church clubs and enjoy planning in the fall so we can get the reservations early and camp together. Now that the entire club is retired, we enjoy camping mid-week to avoid crowds.

MICROWAVE ROCKY ROAD FUDGE

Ingredients

1 large bag chocolate chips
1 large bag butterscotch chips
1 C. creamy peanut butter
1 bag (10.5 oz.) miniature marshmallows
1 C. cocktail peanuts

Instructions

Melt chips and peanut butter in large microwave safe bowl for about 2 minutes on high (depends on microwave power). Beat until very smooth. Fold in marshmallows and peanuts. Spread in 9x13 buttered pan. Refrigerate for at least an hour before cutting.

Barbara Smith, Arroyo Grande, Calif.

I am new to RVing and "hit the road" in August 2010. I have a 37-foot Cardinal 5th wheel. I am a member of Escapees and Good Sam Club. I am currently taking as many educational programs offered by Workamper News as I can fit into my schedule. I have been a home economics educator and truck driver.

SWEET YAM BREAD PUDDING

Ingredients

3 eggs, slightly beaten (1 large)
1 C. milk
⅓ C. packed brown sugar
½ t. pumpkin pie spice
1 t. vanilla extract
1 C. yams, mashed (1 can, 15 oz. size)
3 ½ C. bread cubes
⅓ C. raisins
⅓ C. chopped walnuts
whipped cream for topping (optional)

Instructions

Pre-heat oven to 325 degrees. Combine eggs, milk, brown sugar, pumpkin pie spice, and vanilla in a large bowl. Stir in yams. In an 8x8x2 greased or nonstick baking dish layer bread cubes, raisins, and walnuts. Pour egg mixture over top. Press lightly to moisten all bread. Bake 30-35 minutes or until a knife inserted comes out clean. Serve warm with whipped cream. Also good cold or heated up in the microwave the next day. My husband and I have vanilla yogurt with this instead of whipped cream.

Victoria Jurs, Gold Hill, Ore.

My husband and I have been RVing for 15 years; part of that time has actually been spent living in an RV while traveling, and trying to decide where to relocate. We have had a few different RVs since that time and now own a 2004 33-foot Century Skyline 5th wheel by Nomad.

THREE BERRY PUDDING CAKE

Ingredients

Sugar-free angel food cake (I get it already baked from the store)
1 large box of sugar-free vanilla pudding
1 small container of sugar-free nondairy whip topping
1 bag of 3 types of frozen berries
milk

Instructions

First, thaw the whip topping in fridge overnight. Next, mix pudding according to box. You can save out ¼ cup of whip topping for decoration on top. Fold the whip topping into pudding. Now tear up the cake and put half into the container of choice. (I put it into a glass bowl so you can see the nice mix). You now will layer it using cake, berries, and ending with pudding mix.

Tina Praesel, Orange, Texas

GRILLED PINEAPPLE BOAT

Ingredients

whole fresh pineapple
brown sugar (alternative: half Splenda
and half brown sugar)

Instructions

Slice pineapple into fourths. (Note: Leave top leaves on
and cut through top. This makes for attractive serving.)
Trim out center core. Pat brown sugar on pineapple and
place sugar side down onto hot gas or charcoal grill. Grill
for 2-3 minutes or until pineapple is heated slightly and
sugar melts and caramelizes. Remove from grill and serve.

tech tip

The smell in propane is
added for leak detection
purposes. It is called ethyl
mercaptan.

Normie, Arizona

RV AND CAMPING ORGANIZATIONS AND CLUBS

UNITED STATES & CANADA

Acadiana Ramblers
www.acadianaramblers.org

Airstream Central
www.airstreamcentral.com

AlfaSeeYas
(858) 822-8468
www.alfaseeyas.com

Alpine Coach Association
(509) 457-4133
www.alpinecoachassociation.com

American Clipper Owners Club
(510) 794-9882
www.americanclipperownersclub.com

Archway Coachmen
www.archwaycoachmen.com

Arizona Holiday Rambler Recreation Vehicle Club
www.azhrrvc.org

National Association of RV Parks and Campgrounds (ARVC)
(303) 681-0401
www.arvc.org

Automate RV Club - California
www.automatervclub.com

Avion / Fleetwood Travelcade
(574) 267-6020
my.execpc.com/~drg/avion.html

Beaver Ambassador Club
www.beaveramb.org

Bounders United Inc.
(513) 922-3131
www.bounder.net

Bounders of America
www.bounder.org

Cajun Travelers
www.cajuntravelersrv.com

California Recreation Vehicle Dealers
Association
(916) 791-3021
www.rvingca.org

Camp Club USA
(800) 416-7813

Camping Friends
www.campingfriends.21.forumer.com

Cardinal RV Club
www.cardinalrvclub.org

Carolina Jaybirds Flight 108
www.flight108.com

Casita Travel Club Forum
www.casitaclub.com

CAT RV Club
www.catrvclub.org

Cedar Creek RV Club
www.cedarcreekrvclub.com

Cedar Creek RV Owners Club
www.cedarcreekrvownersclub.com

C'est la Vie Campers
www.cestlaviecampers.com

Circle City Campers
www.circlecitycampers.com

Coachmen Owners Association
(574) 825-8245
(888) 422-2582
www.coachmencaravanclub.com

Coastal Tarheels
www.coastaltarheels.com

Colorado RV Association
(719) 596-2716
www.crva.org

Discovery International
(270) 388-6132
www.difmca.com

Discovery Owners Association
(888) 594-6818
www.discoveryowners.com

East Tennessee Camping Club
www.etncc.5.forumer.com

Escapees RV Club
(888) 757-2582 or (936) 327-8873
www.escapees.com

Family Motor Coach Association
www.fmca.com

Four Winds International
(574) 266-1111
www.thormotorcoach.com

Freightliner Chassis Owners Club
(321) 704-0695
www.fcocrv.org

Explorer RV Club - Canada
(800) 999-0819
www.explorer-rvclub.com

Family Campers and RVers
(716) 668-6242 or (800) 245-9755
www.fcrv.org

Florida PopUp Campers
www.floridapopupcampers.com

Florida RV Trade Association
(813) 741-0488
www.frvta.org

GMC Motorhome Clubs
www.gmcmotorhomes.com

GMC Western States Club
www.gmcws.org

Go RVing
www.gorving.com

Good Sam Club
(800) 234-3450
www.goodsamclub.com

Great Lakes RV Association
(216) 891-9030

Gulf Streamers International RV Club
(800) 289-8787 ext. 3664
www.streamers.gulfstreamcoach.com

Handicapped Travel Club
(305) 230-0687
(305) 987-5329
www.handicappedtravelclub.com

Happy Camper Half Price Camping Club
www.camphalfprice.com

Heartland Owners Club
(574) 262-5992
www.heartlandrvs.com

Highland Rim Travelers
www.highlandrimtravelers.com

Hitchhikers of America, International
(574) 258-0571
www.hitchhikerrvclub.com

Holiday Rambler Recreational Vehicle Club Inc.
(574) 295-9800
(877) 702-5415
www.hrrvc.org

International Snowbird Travel Club
www.snowbirdclub.homestead.com

Jayco Travel Club
(800) 262-5178
(574) 258-0571 ext. 45
www.jaycorvclub.com

Kentucky Manufactured Housing Institute
(502) 223-0490
www.kmhi.org

Las Vegas Rolling Wheels
easysite.com/lvrollingwheelsrvclub

Lone Star Caravaners
www.orgsites.com/tx/lscc/

Louisiana RV Association, Inc.
(318) 235-8547

Marina Village Resort
(936) 594-3805 or (800) 392-3330
www.marina-village.com

Maryland RV Dealers Association
(410) 987-6300
www.mdrv.com

Michigan Manufactured Housing, RV
& Campground Association
(517) 349-8881

Monaco International RV Club
www.monacointernationalrvclub.com

Monaco Northeast Explorers
www.monaconortheastexplorers.com

Monaco RV Club
www.monacorvclub.com

Monacos In Motion
www.monacosinmotion.org

Monaco Romers
www.monacoromers.com

Montana Manufactured Housing
& RV Association
(406) 442-2164
www.mtmhrv.org

Montana Owners Club
www.montanaowners.com

North American Family Campers Association
NAFCA Bay Path 114
www.baypath114.tripod.com

NAFCA Berkshire 10
www.berkshire10nafca.tripod.com

NAFCA Canvasback 157
(978) 664-4294
www.canvasback157.tripod.com

NAFCA Orlando 183
www.orlando183nafca.tripod.com

NAFCA Site Seekers 51
(413) 245-9693
www.siteseekers51.tripod.com

NAFCA Springfield 1
www.nafca.org/springfield

National African-American RV'ers Association
(704) 333-3070
www.naarva.com

National RV Central States Club
www.nationalrv-centralstates.org

National Camping Travelers
www.gonct.org/index1.html

Newmar Kountry Klub
(574) 773-7791
(877) 639-5582
www.newmarkountryklub.com

New York Centrals
www.newyorkcentrals.com

North Coast Family Campers
www.freewebs.com

Northeast Florida Camping Club
www.neflcc.com

Northwood RV Owners Association
www.afnash.com

NSF International
(734) 769-8010
www.nsf.org

Ohio Nomads
(937) 275-8574
www.ohionomads.com

Pacific Trailer Club
www.beamalarm.com

Palm Tree 27
(608) 504-4914
www.nafca.org

Passport America
(800) 681-6810
www.passportamerica.com

Pennsylvania RV & Camping Association
(717) 303-0295
www.prvca.org

The Pioneer Camping Club
(408) 568-8837
www.pioneercampingclub.com

Pioneer Valley 8
(413) 781-CAMP (2267)
www.springfieldrvcampingshow.com

Quahaug 48
www.angelfire.com

Recreational Park Trailer Industry Association
(770) 251-2672
www.rptia.org

Recreation Vehicle Indiana Council
(317) 247-6258
www.campindiana.com

Resort Camplands International
(860) 774-7885
www.resortcamplands.com

Roadtrek Owners' Club
www.roadtrekchapter.org

Roaming Elks #1082
www.users.techline.com/elks1082/trlr.htm

RV Dealers Association
(703) 591-7130
www.rvda.org

RVing Women
(888) 557-8464
www.rvingwomen.com

RV Rentals Association
(703) 359-0152
www.rvra.org

Safari-International
(352) 360-5478
www.safari-international.org

San Jose Run-A-Bouts
www.sanjoserunabouts.org

South California Touring Tears
(760) 369-3082
www.teardroptours.com

Southwest Bluebirds
www.southwest-bluebirds.org

SOI Club
(818) 249-4023, ext. 215
www.soiclub.com

Squaw-No-Cook 30
www.snc30nafca.tripod.com

Starcraft Camper Club
(800) 262-5178 or (574) 258-0571 ext. 43
www.starcraftrvclub.com/

Sunny Brook RV Club
(800) 262-5178 or (574) 258-0571 ext. 42
www.sunnybrookrvclub.com

Streamline Royal Rovers-Houston
www.tompatterson.com/Streamline/Streamline.html

Texas Boomers RV Club
www.texasboomers.net

Texas Recreational Vehicle Association
(512) 327-4514
www.trva.org

Texas "Free Spirit" Camping Club
www.texasfreespiritcampingclub.org

Thousand Trails
(800) 205-0606
www.thousandtrails.com

TrailManor Trailblazers Club
www.trailmanor.com

Travelin' Tarheels
www.travelintarheels.com

Travlin' Texans
www.travlin-texans.org

Truck Cap & Accessories Association
(703) 922-7803

United Motorcoach Association
(800) 424-8262
www.uma.org

Vintage Airstream Club
www.vintageairstreamclub.com

Virginia Campers
www.vacampers.com

Volunteer Campers
www.volunteercampers.com

Wally Byam Caravan Club International
(937) 596-5211
www.wbcci.org

Western Bus Nuts
(916) 481-2781
www.fmcawbn.com

Western Slope Rovers
www.westernsloperovers.com

Westfalia Owners
www.westfalia.org

Winnebago-Itasca Travelers Club
(800) 643-4892
www.winnebagoind.com/clubs/wit

West Virginia Recreational Vehicle Association
(304) 727-7441

Workamper News
(800) 446-5627
www.workamper.com

INDEX

RVERS CONTRIBUTING RECIPES

ACKNOWLEDGEMENTS

First, I do all things in the name of Jesus Christ, my Savior and Redeemer.

Second, a very special thank you goes out to my husband and best friend, Terry Cooper, who gives me his love and encouragement in all things my heart desires.

Also, I would like to thank the Recreation Vehicle Industry Association (RVIA) for endorsing this publication as the official RV centennial cookbook in celebration of 100 years of RVing.

This book is dedicated to the moms and dads who RV with their children; those who manage the thousands of RV parks and campgrounds; the ones who spend long, hard hours managing and working in the RV dealerships and service departments; the genius minds of those who design and build the RVs; to all the special groups, clubs and organizations.

Thank you to all who, in the last century, have helped make the RV industry what it is today.

Evada Cooper

ABOUT THE AUTHOR

Early in life, Evada Cooper managed to combine her interest in the food industry with her love of RVing. At the age of 27, Evada opened a deli in her hometown of Rockdale, Texas. During the summer, Evada and her daughters would hitch up their pop-up trailer and travel to campgrounds all over Texas and Colorado. As the children grew older, Evada upgraded to a travel trailer, then to a 5th wheel, gaining experience with many different types of RVs. Years later, Evada left the deli business and became a full-time RVer with her teenage daughter as they set out for a new life in Waco, Texas.

Evada met and married Terry Cooper in 2008, and today, the two of them work and live the RVing lifestyle. Terry is a master-certified RV technician and instructor at Texas State Technical College Waco and an online RV technician instructor at Northampton Community College in Bethlehem, Pennsylvania. Terry teaches RV technicians while Evada manages their online business–Mobile RV Academy (mobilervacademy.com). MRVA is a consumer-based training academy specializing in RV maintenance for men and women. Evada and Terry also travel throughout the United States offering RV maintenance seminar training.

Creating this cookbook helped Evada combine her passion for RVing with her love for "family, friends and food."

Evada says, "This cookbook represents all those who have come before us. What an honor to be a part of this history."